WOLFGANG AMADEUS MOZART

Four Horn Concertos
and
Concert Rondo

Concerto No. 1 in D Major (K. 412)
Concerto No. 2 in E♭ Major (K. 417)
Concerto No. 3 in E♭ Major (K. 447)
Concerto No. 4 in E♭ Major (K 495)
Concert Rondo in E♭ Major (K. 371)

For Horn and Orchestra

REDUCTION FOR HORN AND PIANO

ALLEGRO
EDITIONS

Published in 2023 by Allegro Editions

Four Horn Concertos and Concert Rondo
ISBN: 978-1-64837-236-0 (casebound)
978-1-64837-237-7 (paperback)

Cover design by Kaitlyn Whitaker

Cover art: French horn by RodrigoBlanco, courtesy of iStock;
Black and White Piano Illustration. 3D render by Nerthuz, courtesy of iStock

Table of Contents

A Word on the Works

Mozart's four horn concertos, written between 1783 and 1791 for the accomplished horn player Joseph Leutgeb, are some of the most famous works in the horn repertoire. They are among the last works Mozart wrote before his untimely death.

The first concerto is perhaps the most famous of the four and is known for its virtuosic solo part and lively outer movements. The second concerto is lyrical and intimate, while the third is expansive and features a particularly beautiful slow movement. The fourth concerto is perhaps the most unique of the four, with its use of a solo horn quartet in the second movement.

One of the most impressive aspects of the horn concertos is the way in which Mozart is able to showcase the unique qualities of the horn as an instrument. In that era the horn had only recently been adapted for use in classical music, and Mozart was one of the first composers to fully exploit its range and timbre. The solo parts in the concertos are particularly challenging, requiring the horn player to execute a wide range of techniques and to navigate complex runs and passages.

Despite their technical demands, the horn concertos are beloved by horn players and audiences alike for their beauty and elegance. They are a testament to Mozart's genius as a composer, and to his ability to elevate even the humblest of instruments to new heights of musical expression.

Concerto No. 1 in D Major

for Horn and Orchestra

[K. 412]

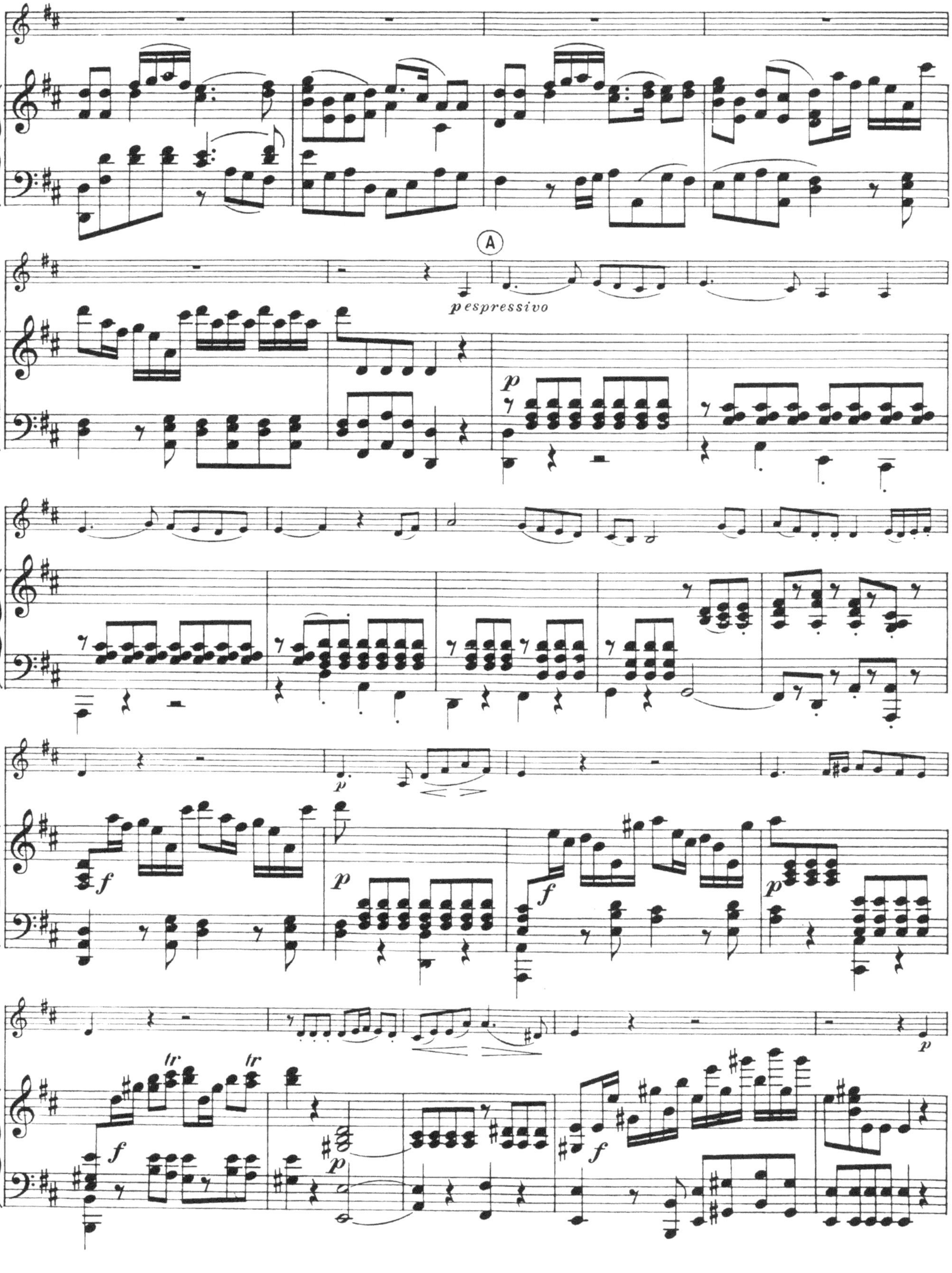
A
pespressivo
p
f
tr

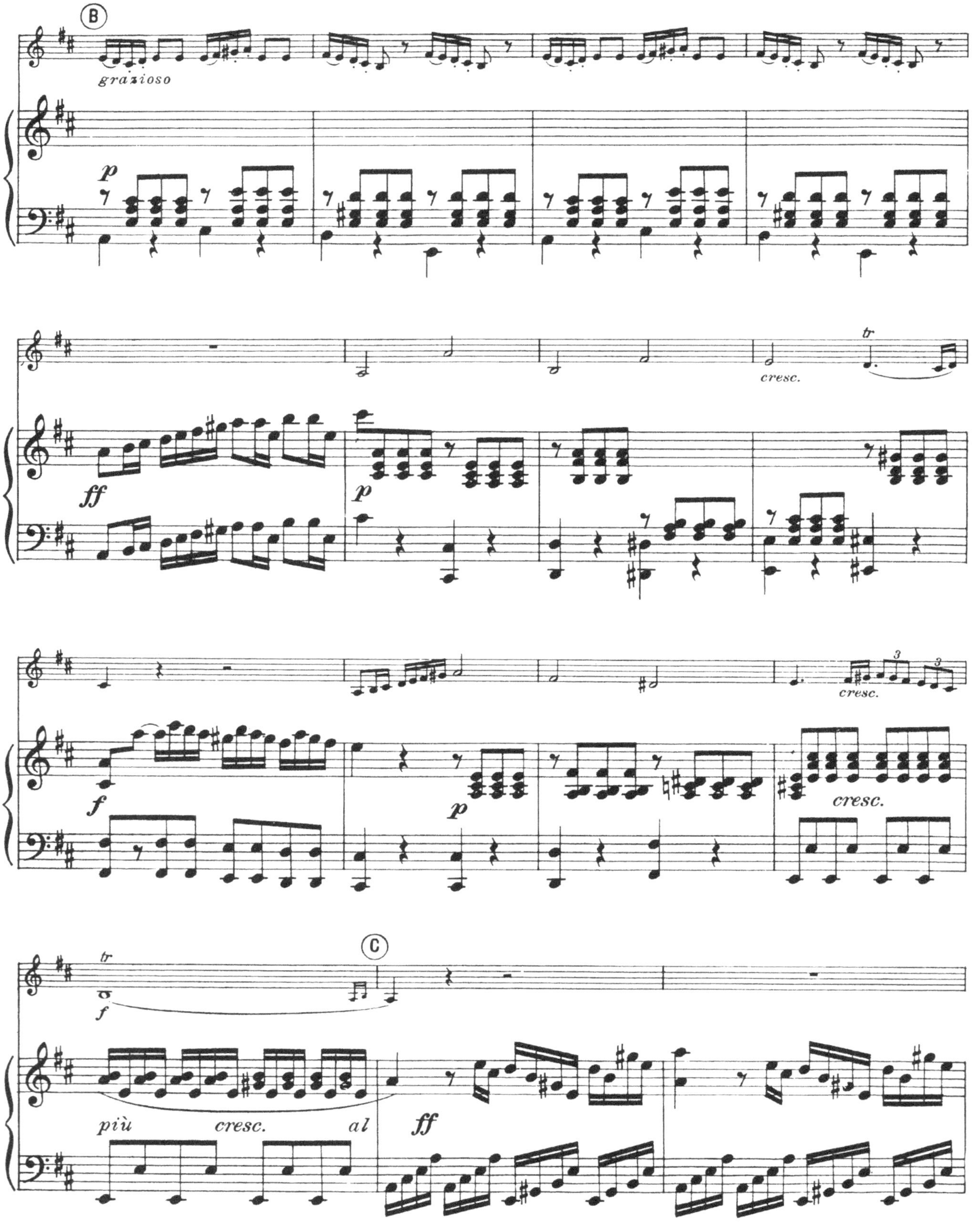
B
grazioso
p
tr
cresc.
ff
p
f
p
cresc.
3
C
f
più cresc. al
ff

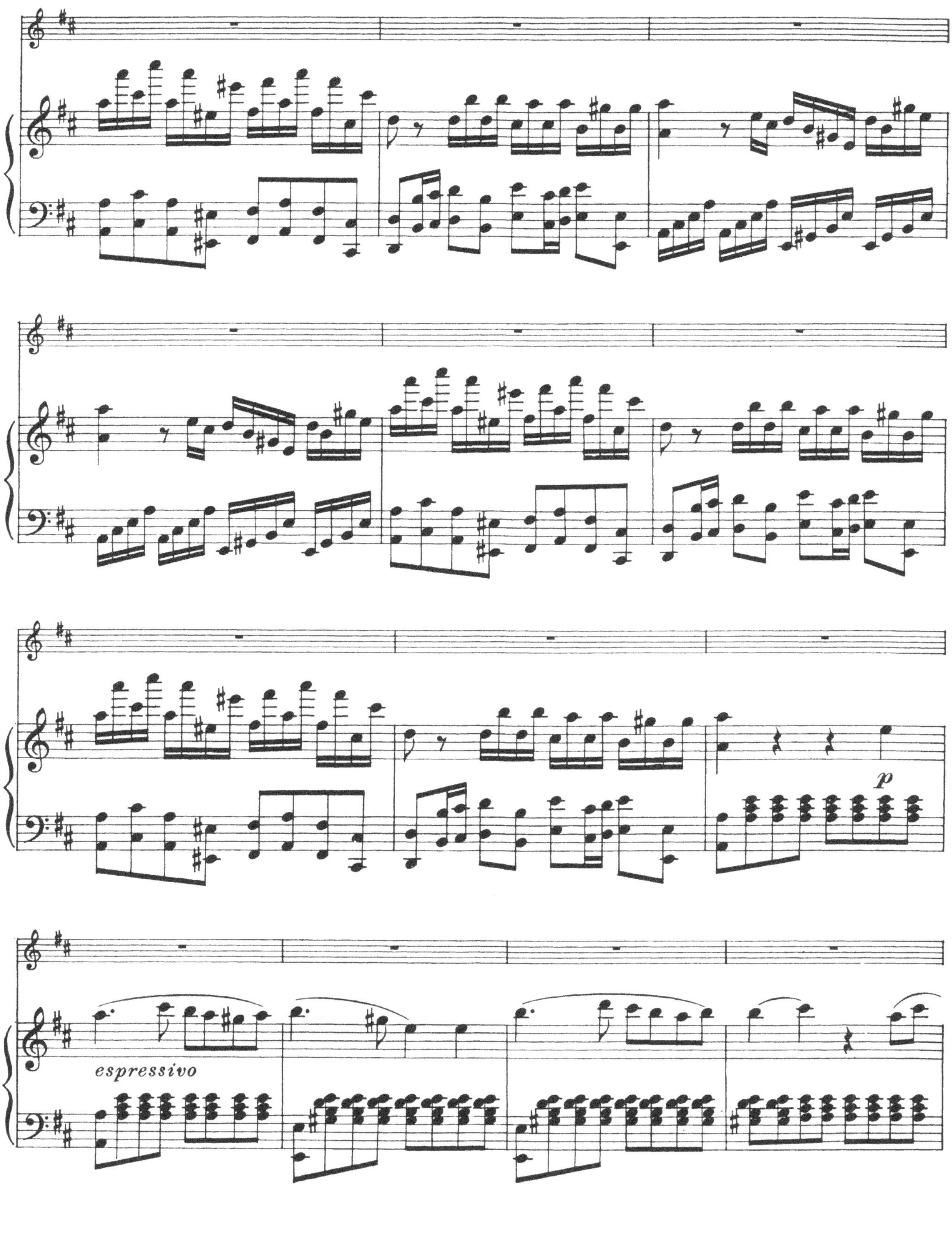
p
espressivo

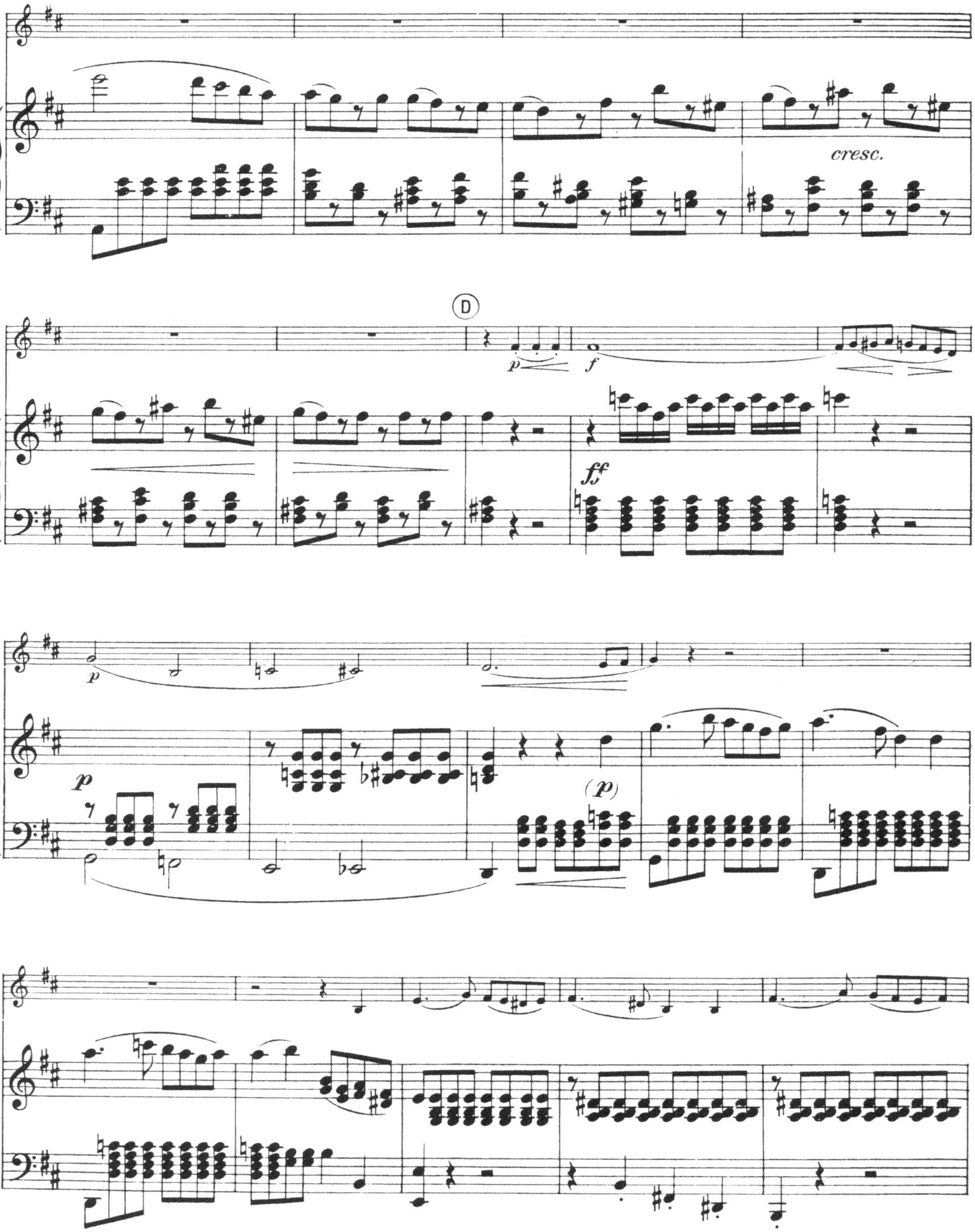
cresc.
D
p
f
ff
p
(p)

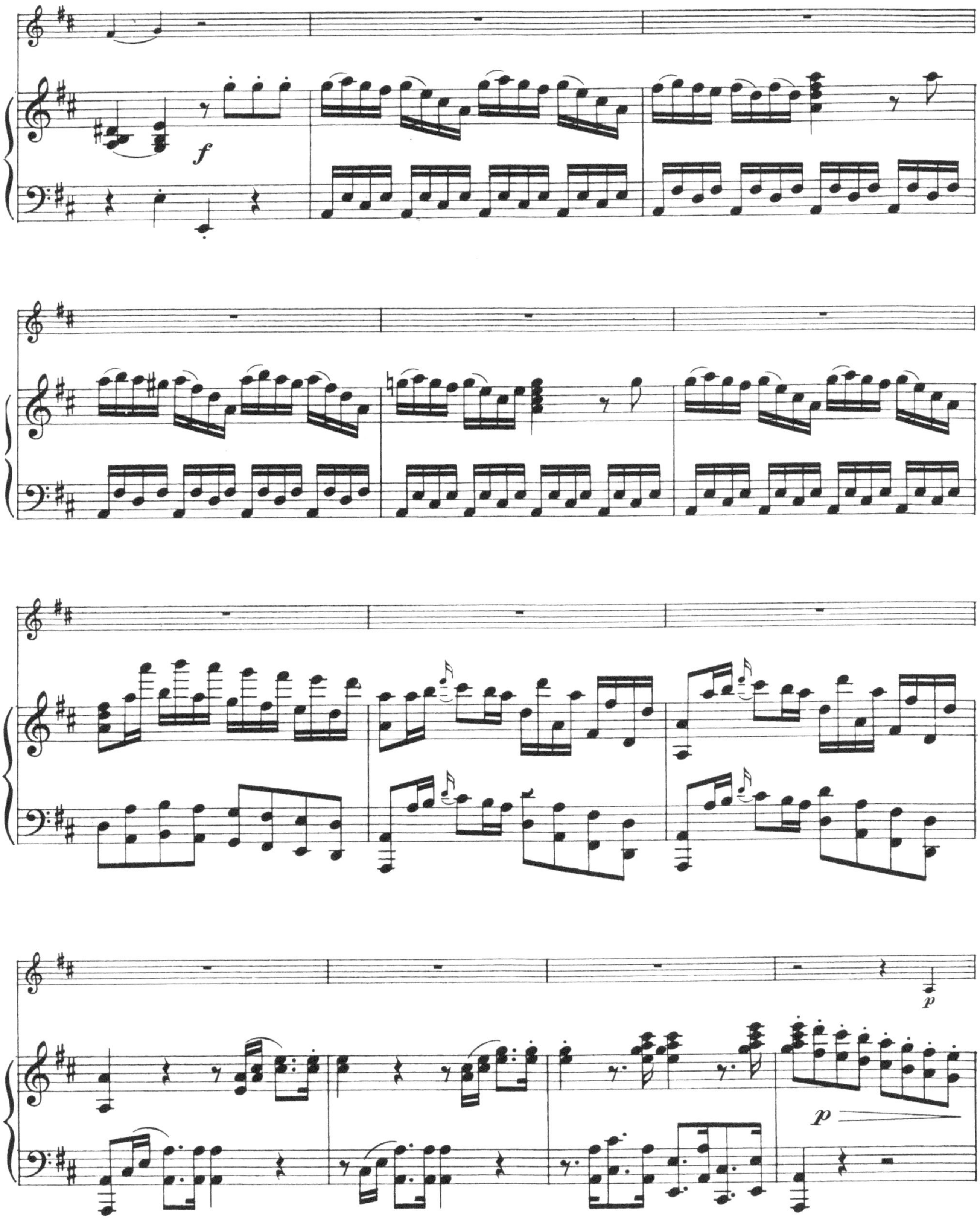
f
p
p

Concerto No. 1 in D Major

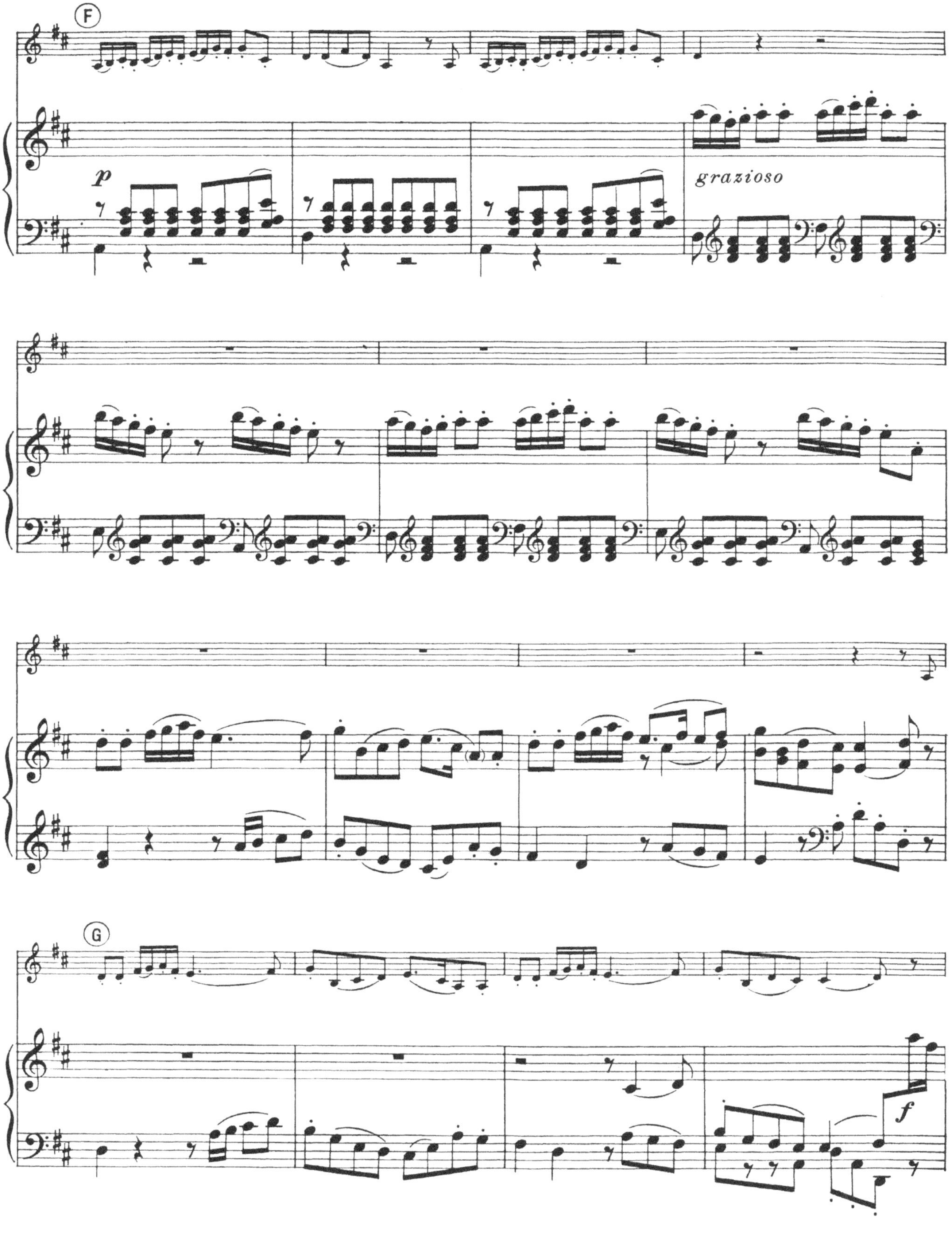
F
p
grazioso
G
f

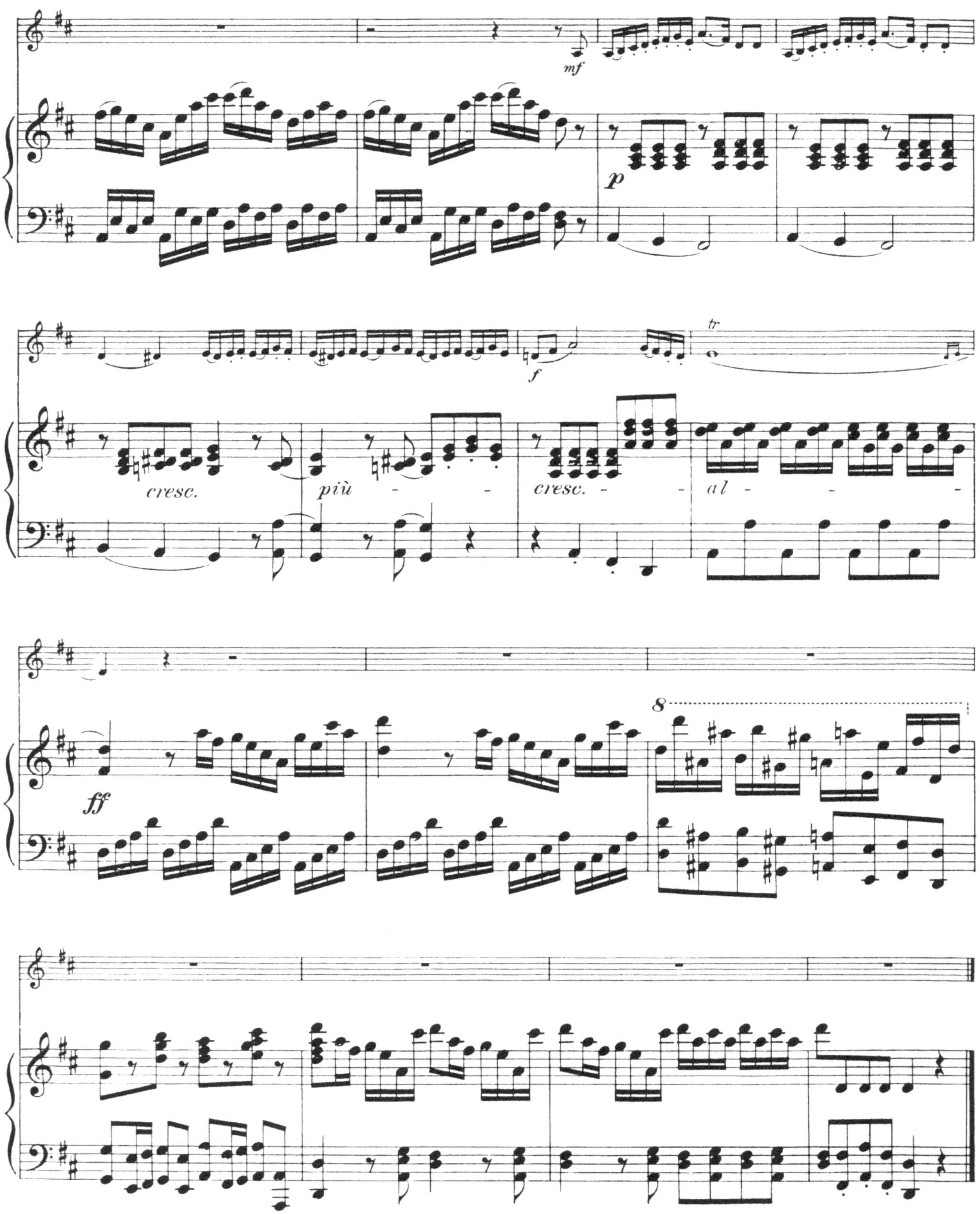
mf
p
cresc.
più
cresc.
al
f
tr
ff
8

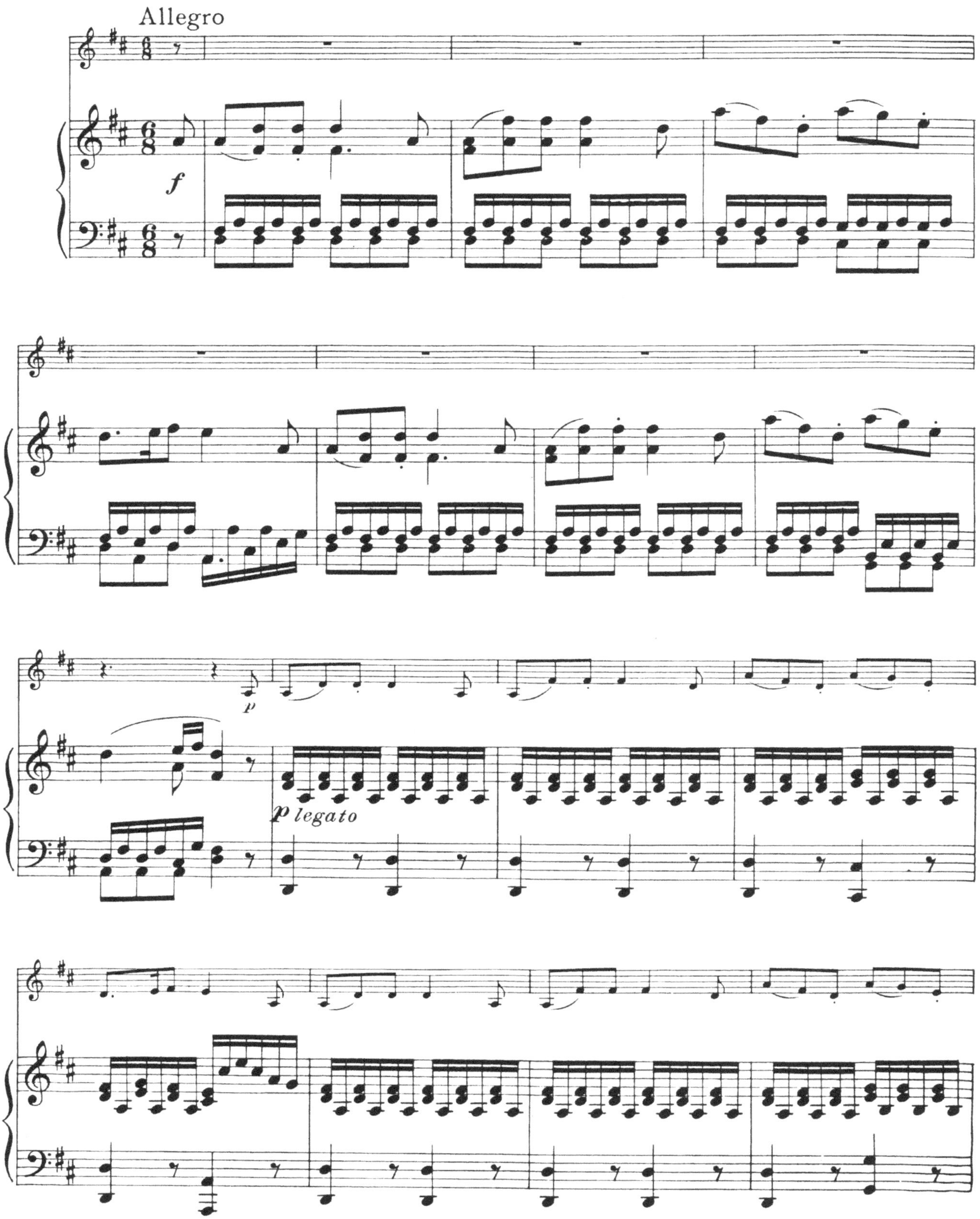
Allegro
f
p
p legato

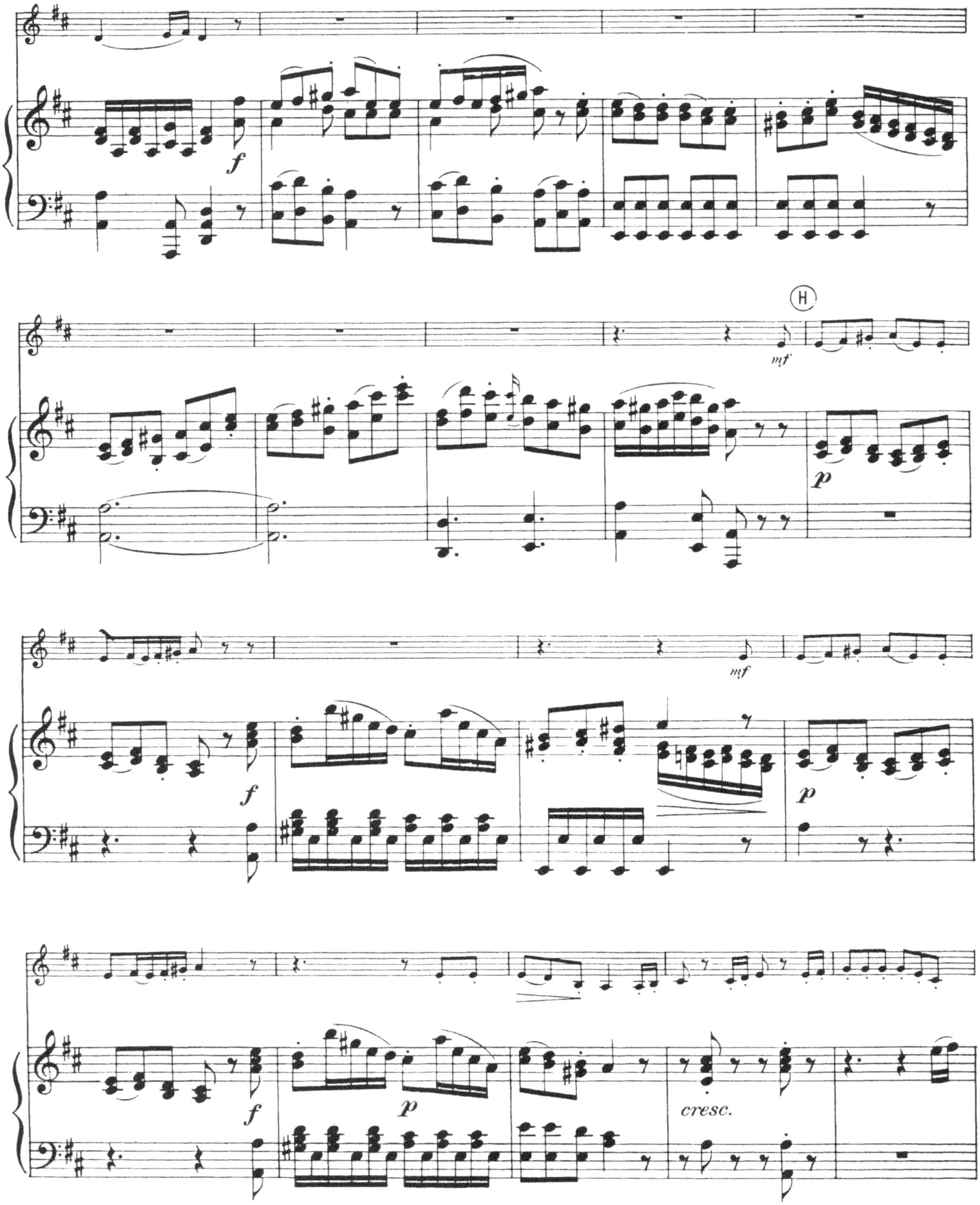
f
H
mf
p
f
mf
p
f
p
cresc.

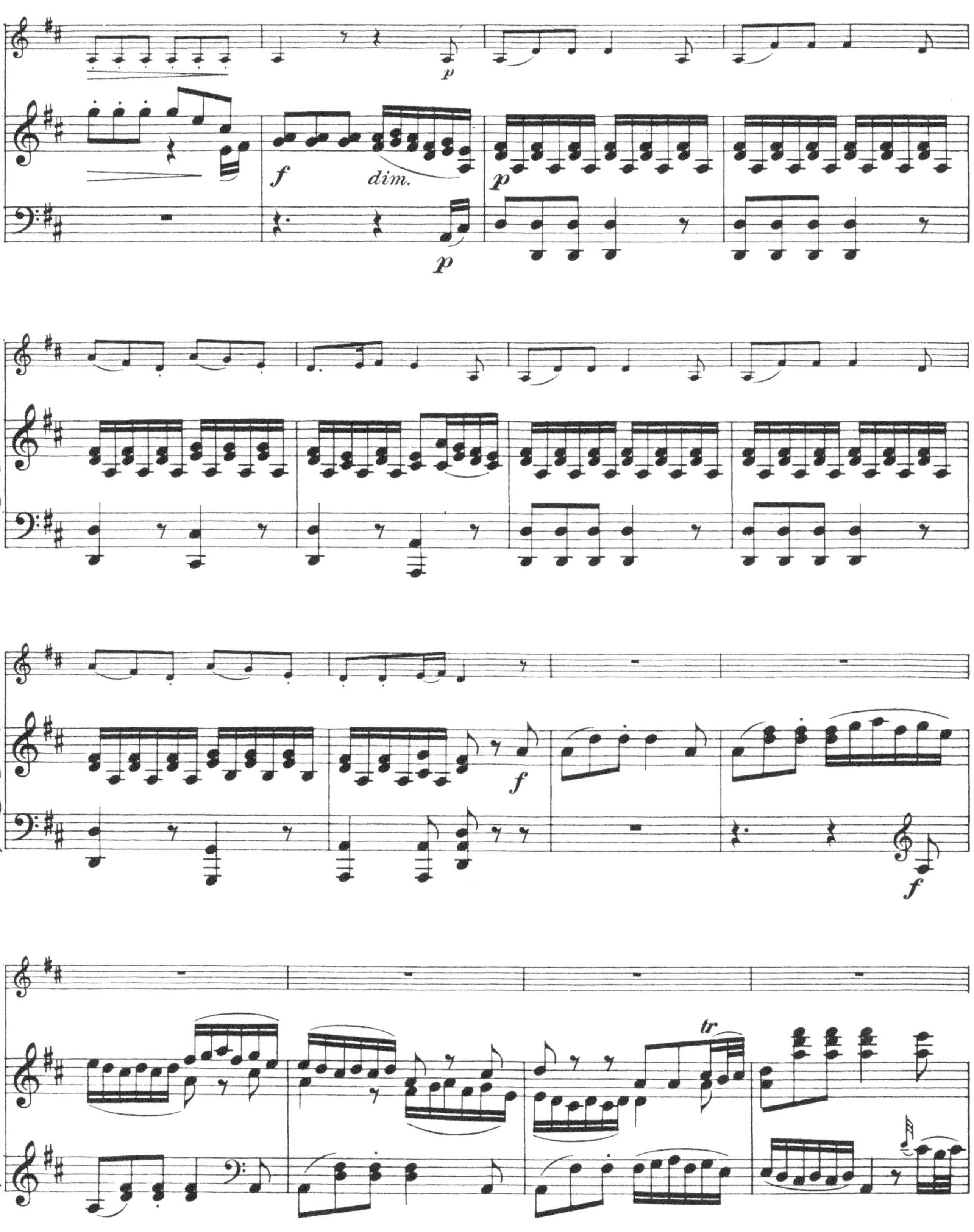
p
f
dim.
p
p
f
f
tr

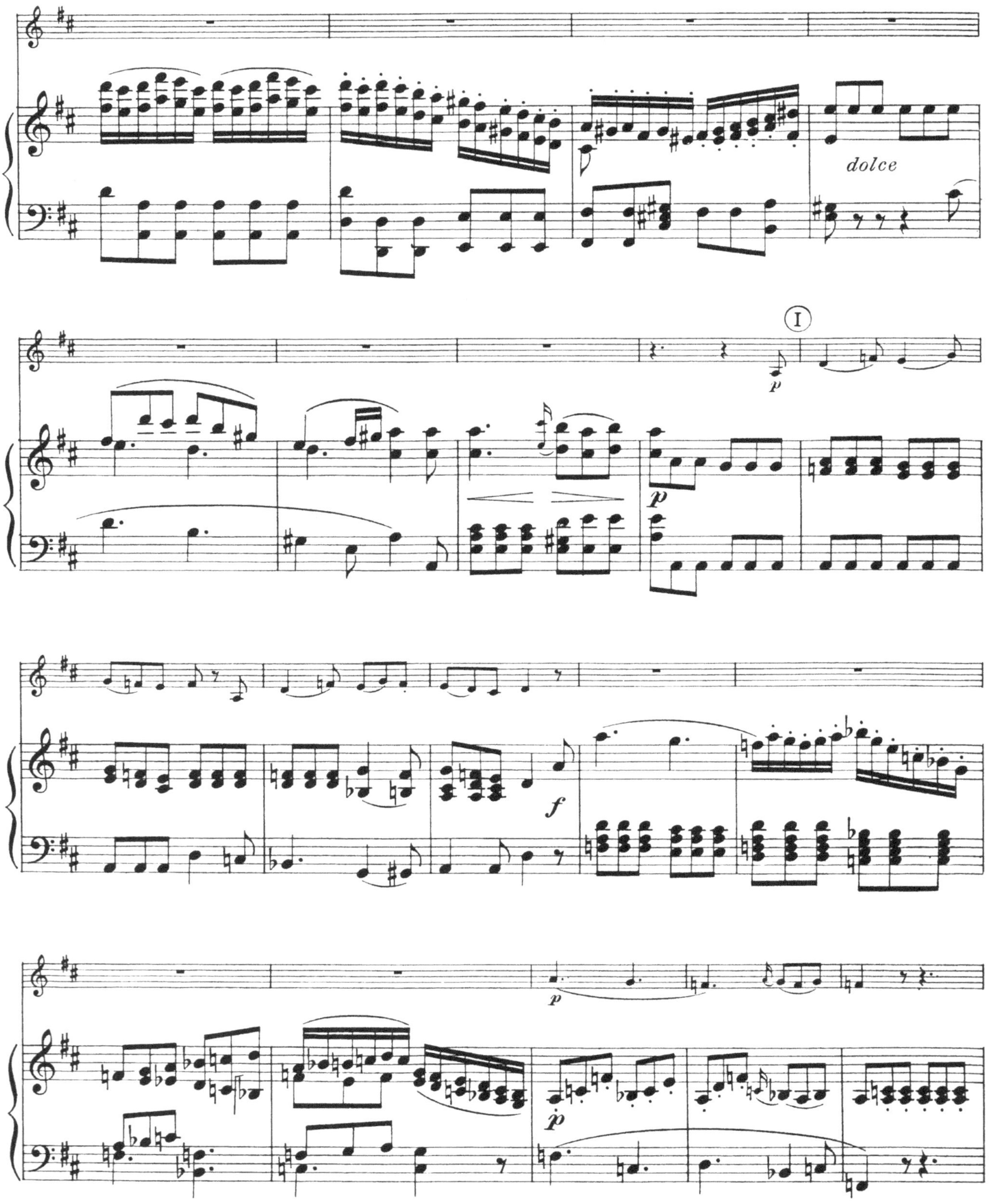
dolce
I
p
p
f
p
p

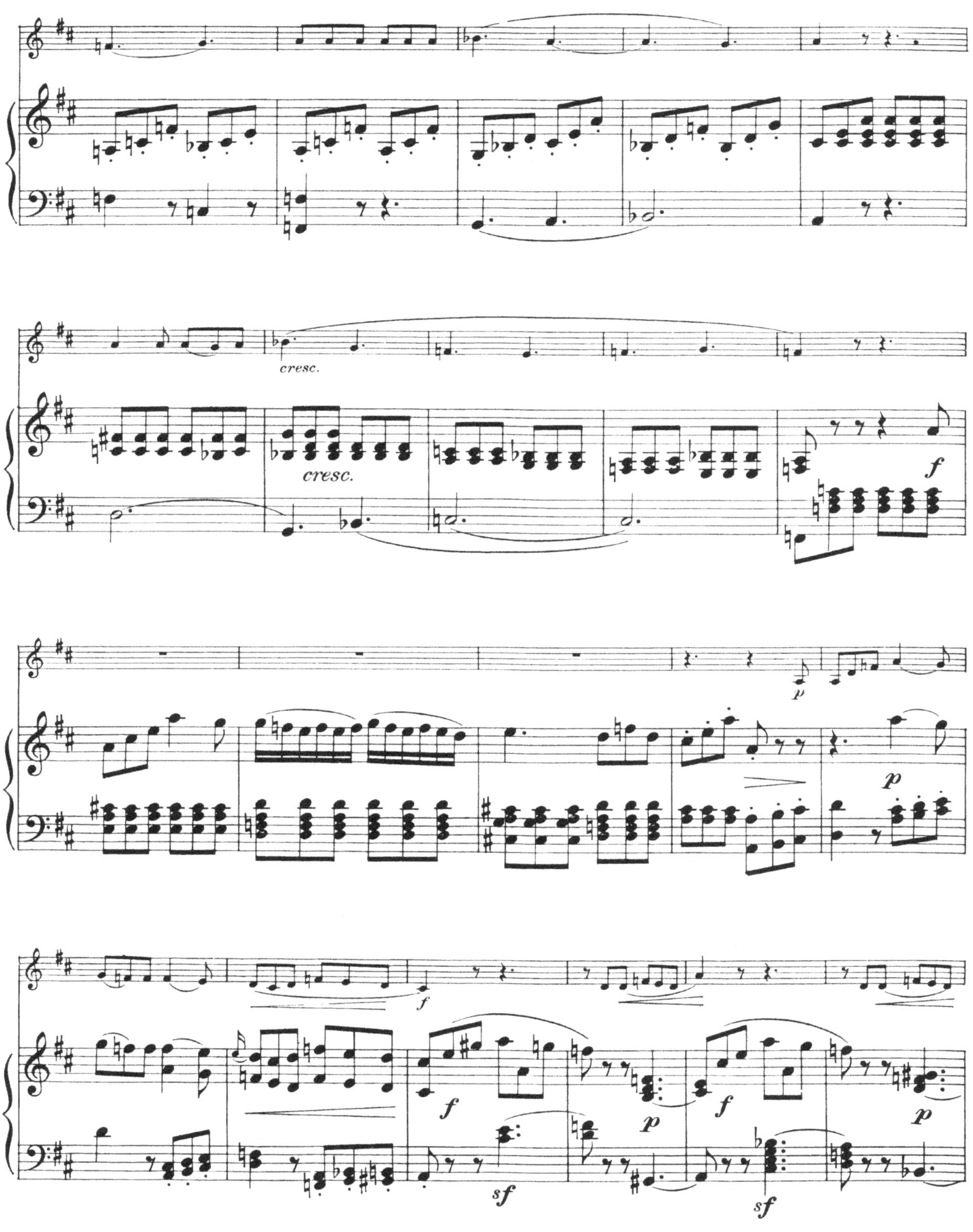
cresc.
cresc.
f
p
p
f
f
sf
p
f
sf
p

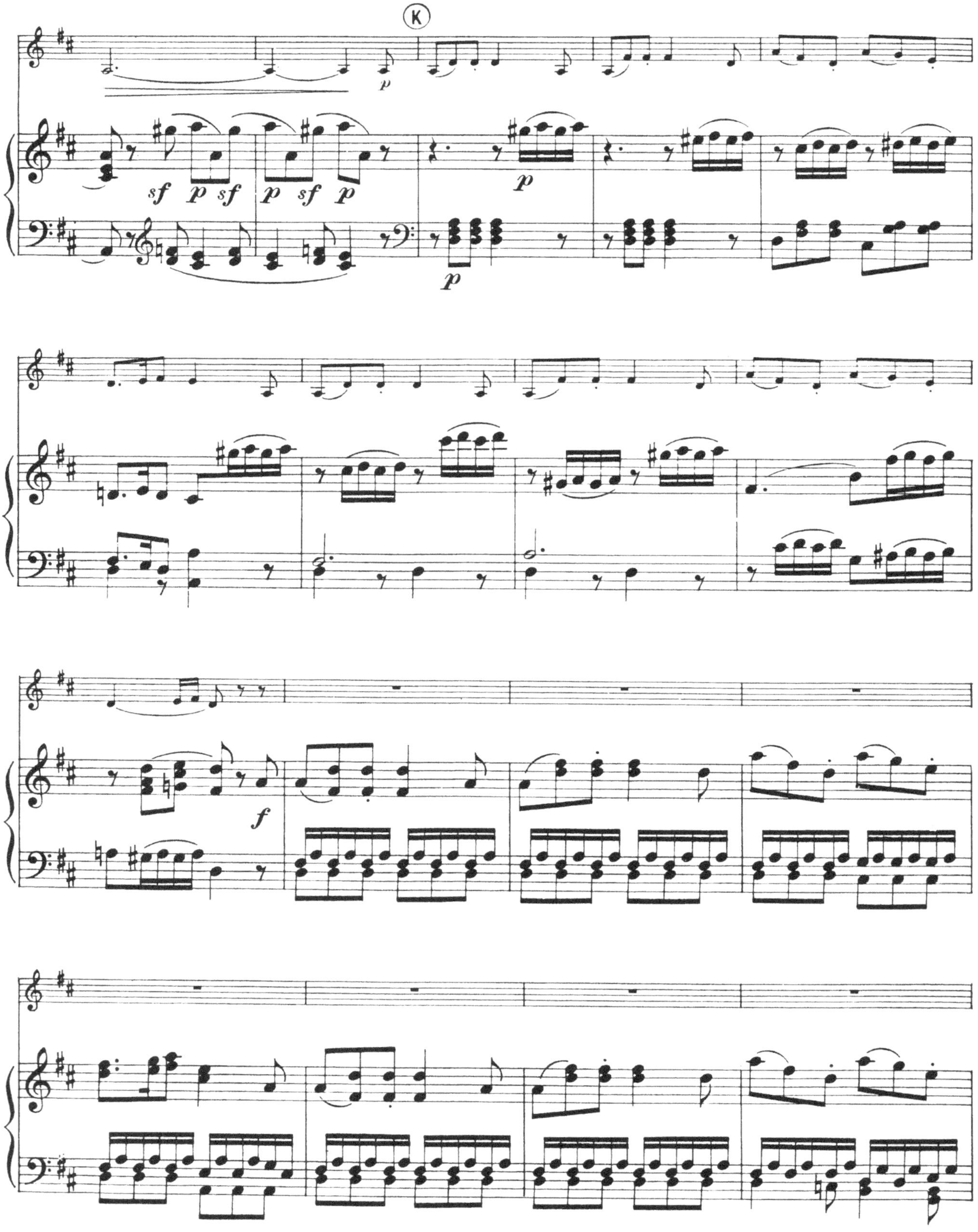
K
p
sf
p
sf
p
sf
p
p
p
f

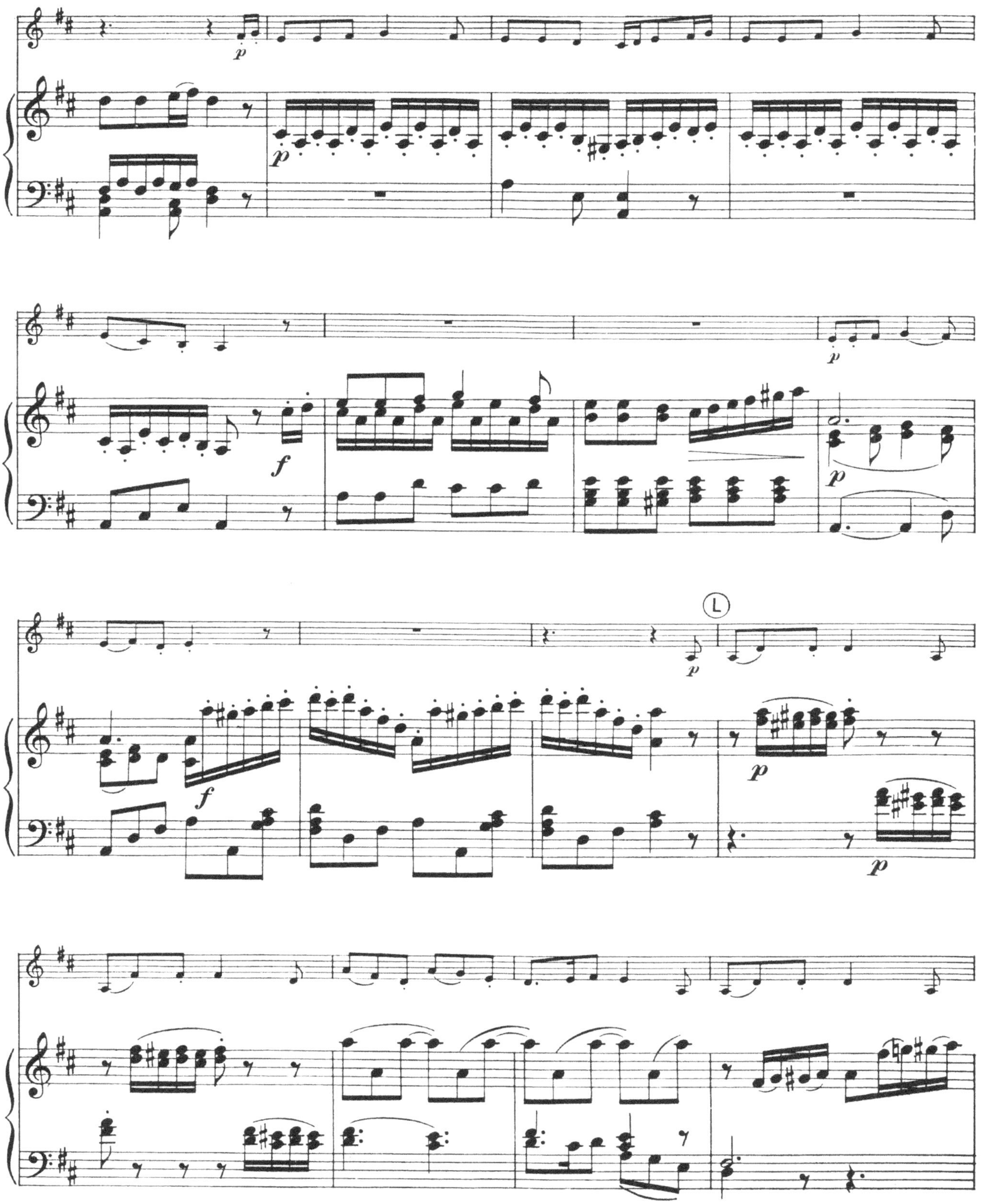
p
p
f
p
L
p
f
p
p

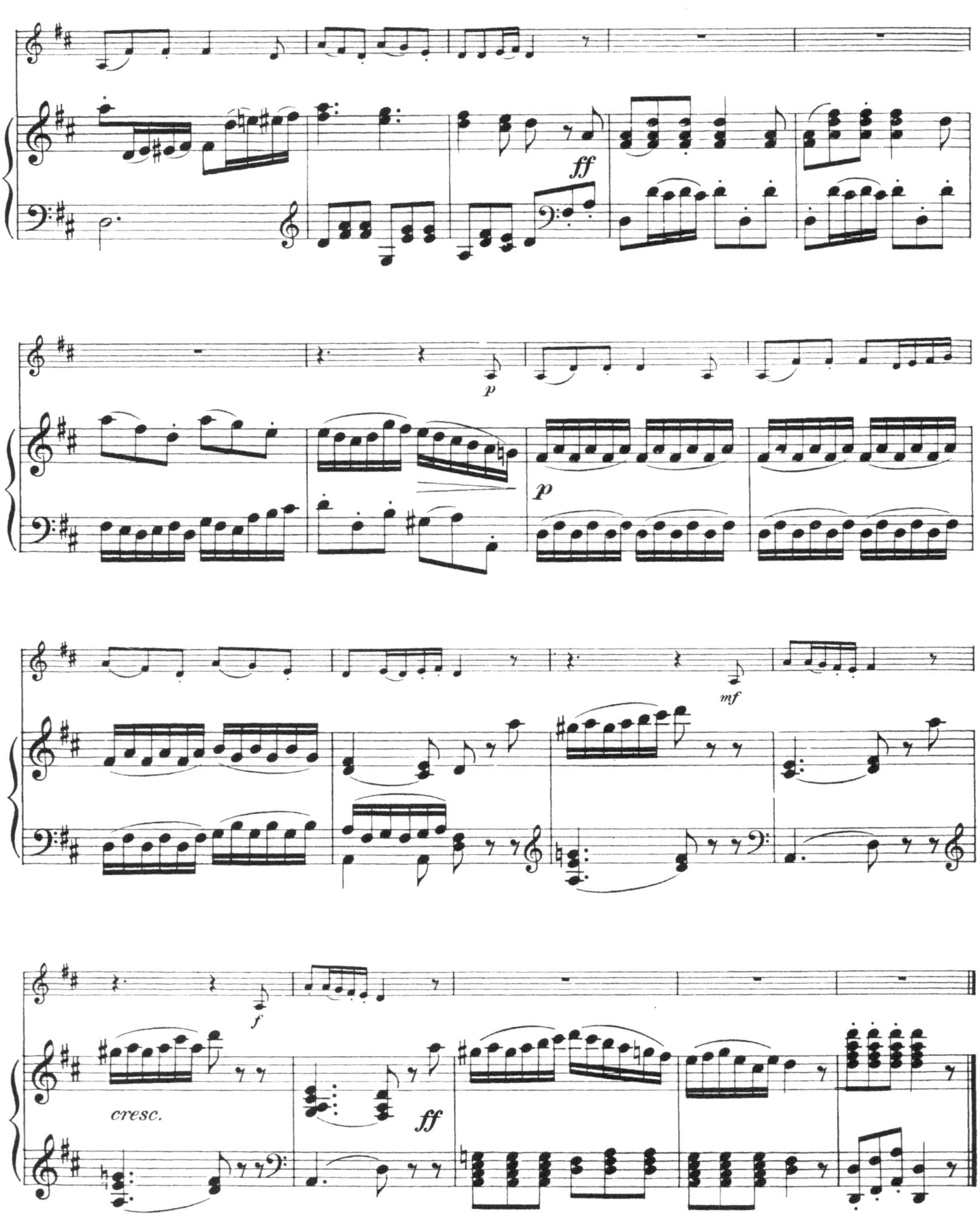
ff
p
p
mf
f
cresc.
ff

Concerto No. 2 in E♭ Major

for Horn and Orchestra

[K. 417]

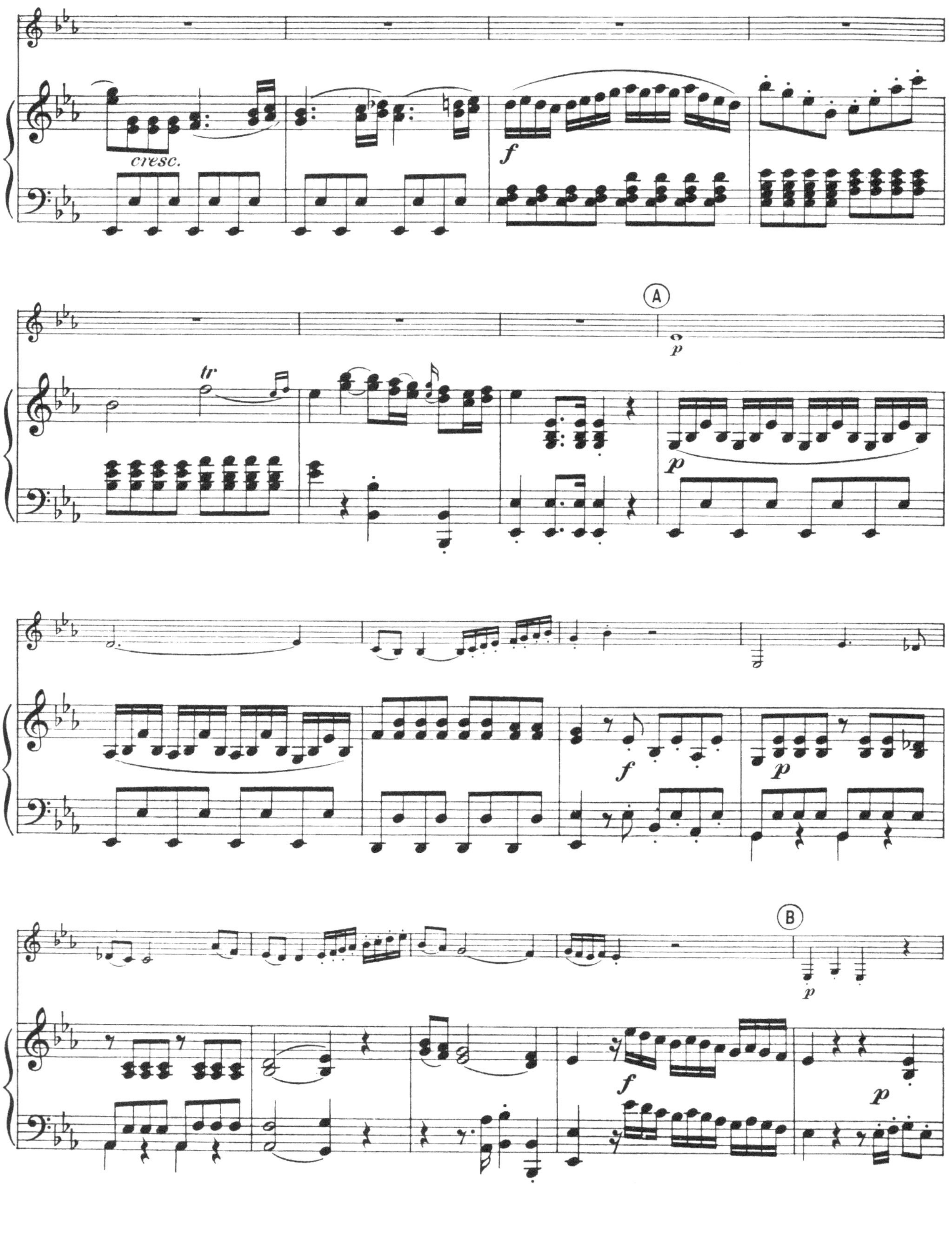
cresc.
tr
A
B

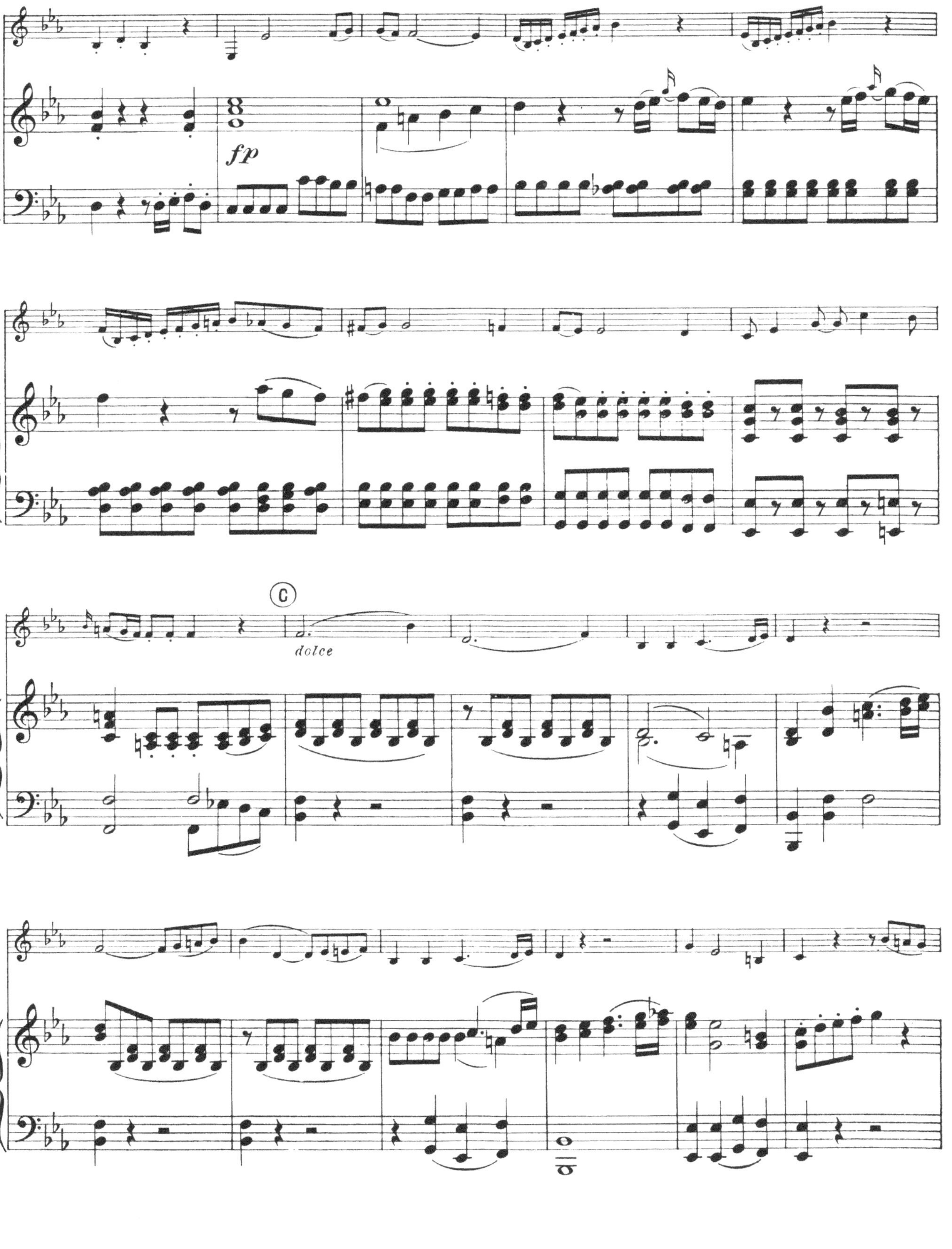
fp
C
dolce

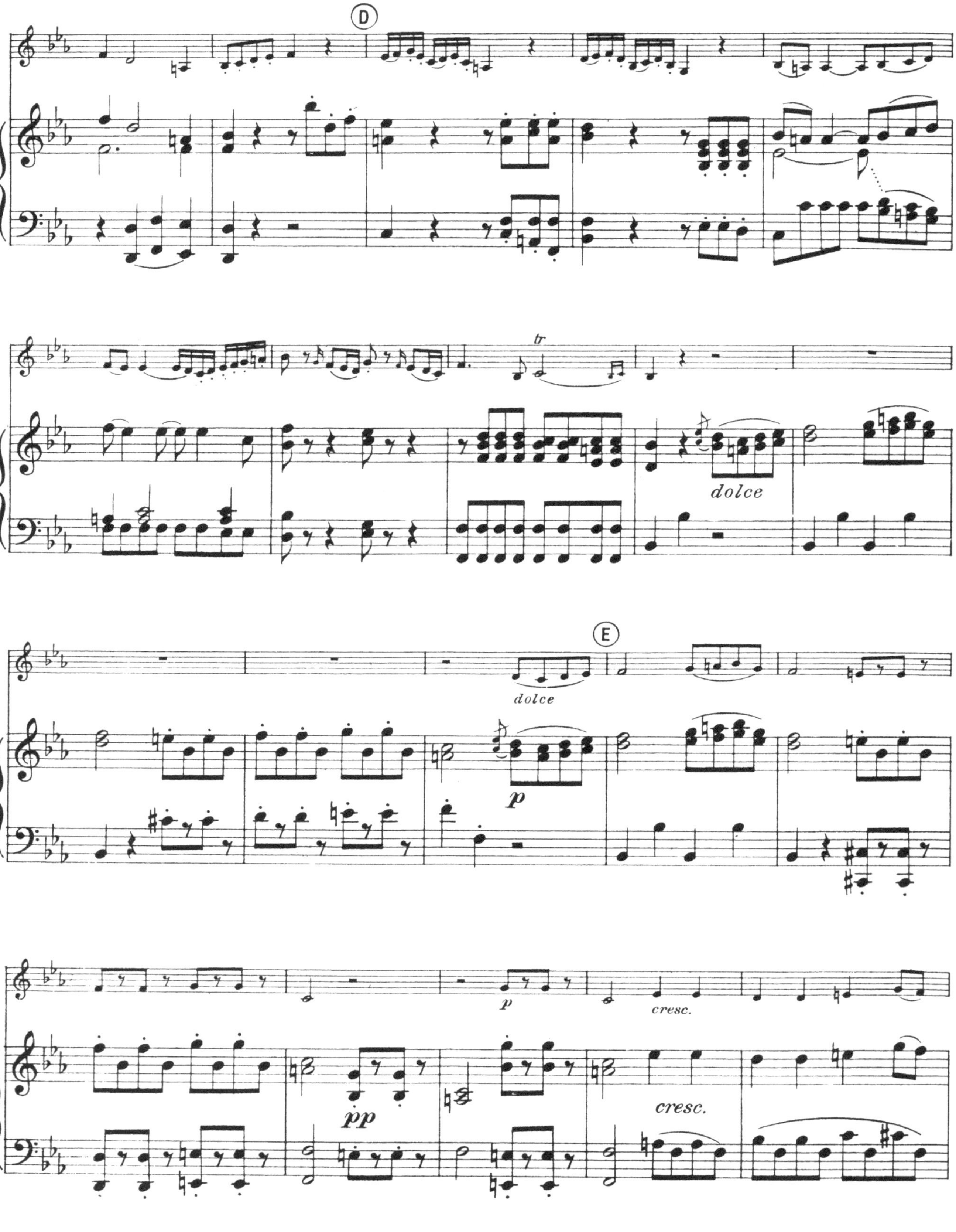
D
tr
dolce
E
dolce
p
p
pp
cresc.
cresc.

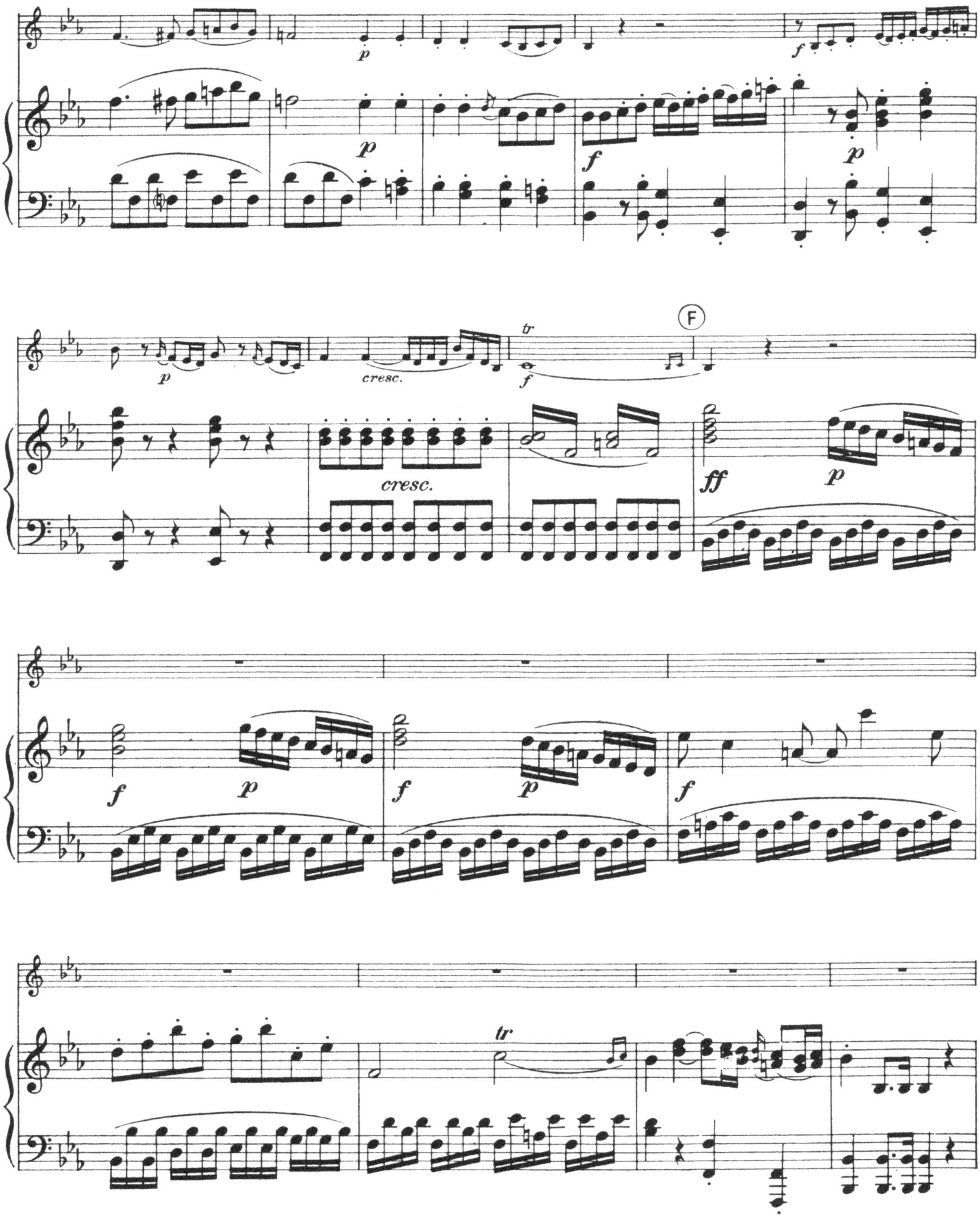
p
f
p
f
p
p
cresc.
cresc.
tr
f
F
ff
p
f
p
f
p
f
tr

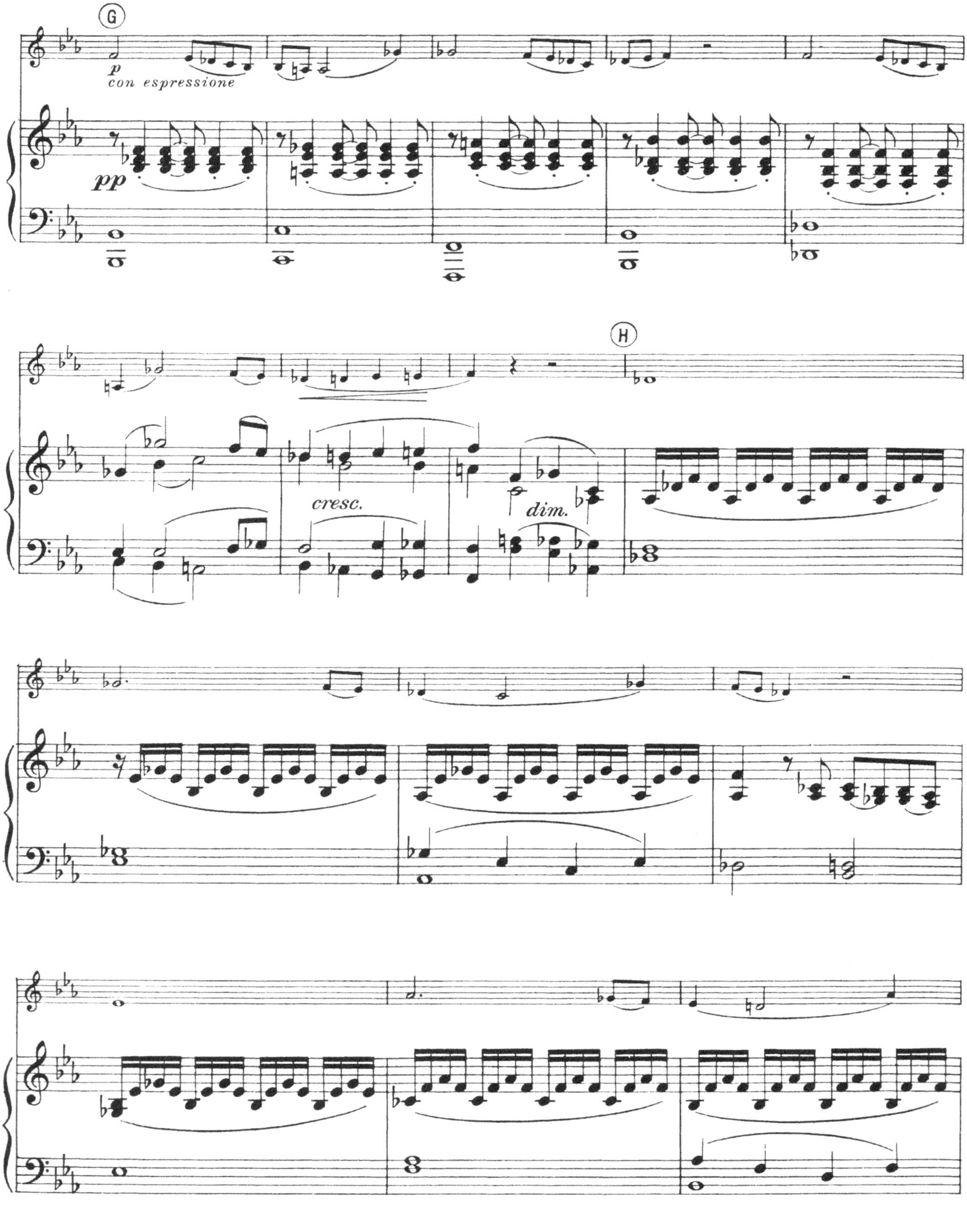
G
p
con espressione
pp
H
cresc.
dim.

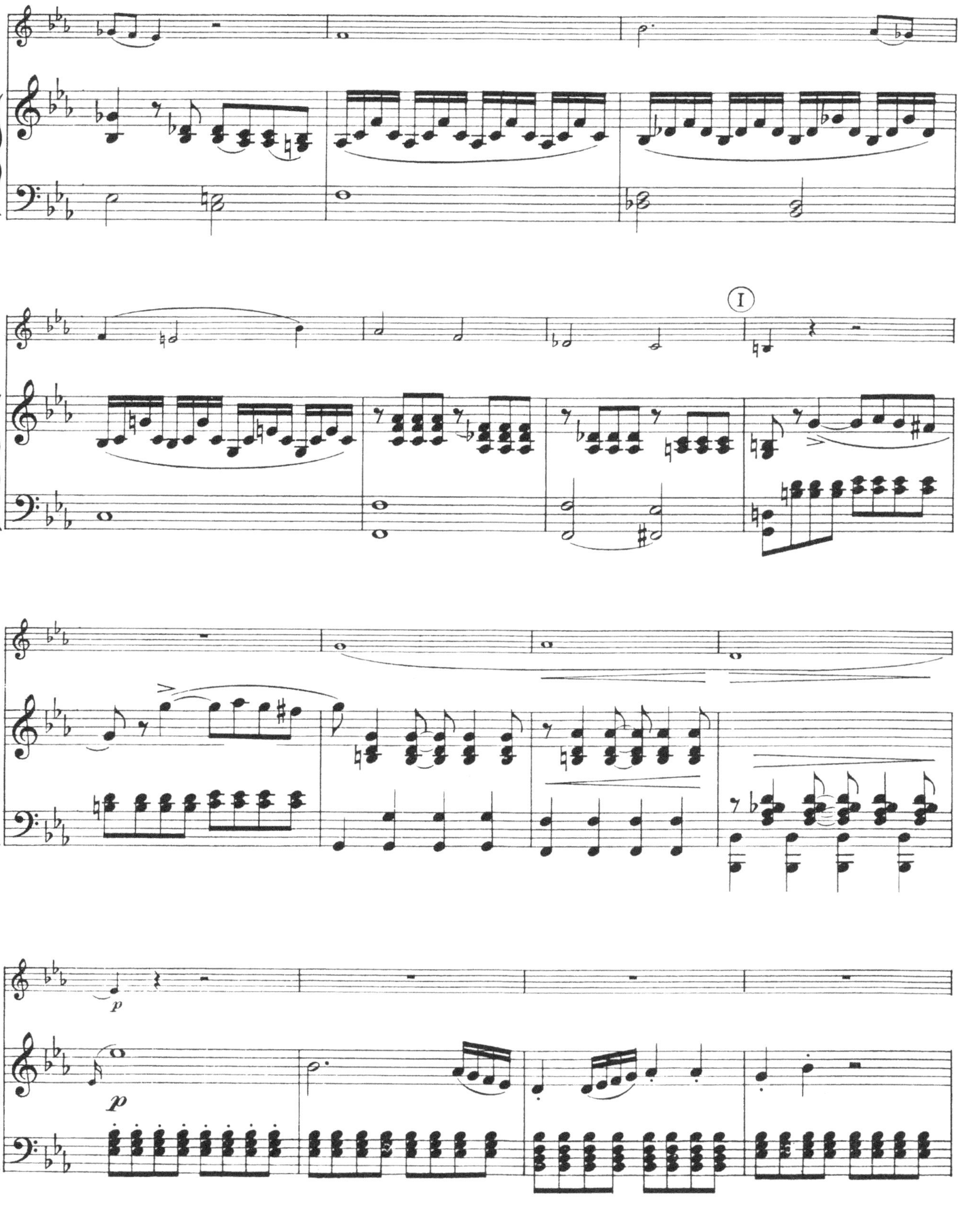
I
p
p

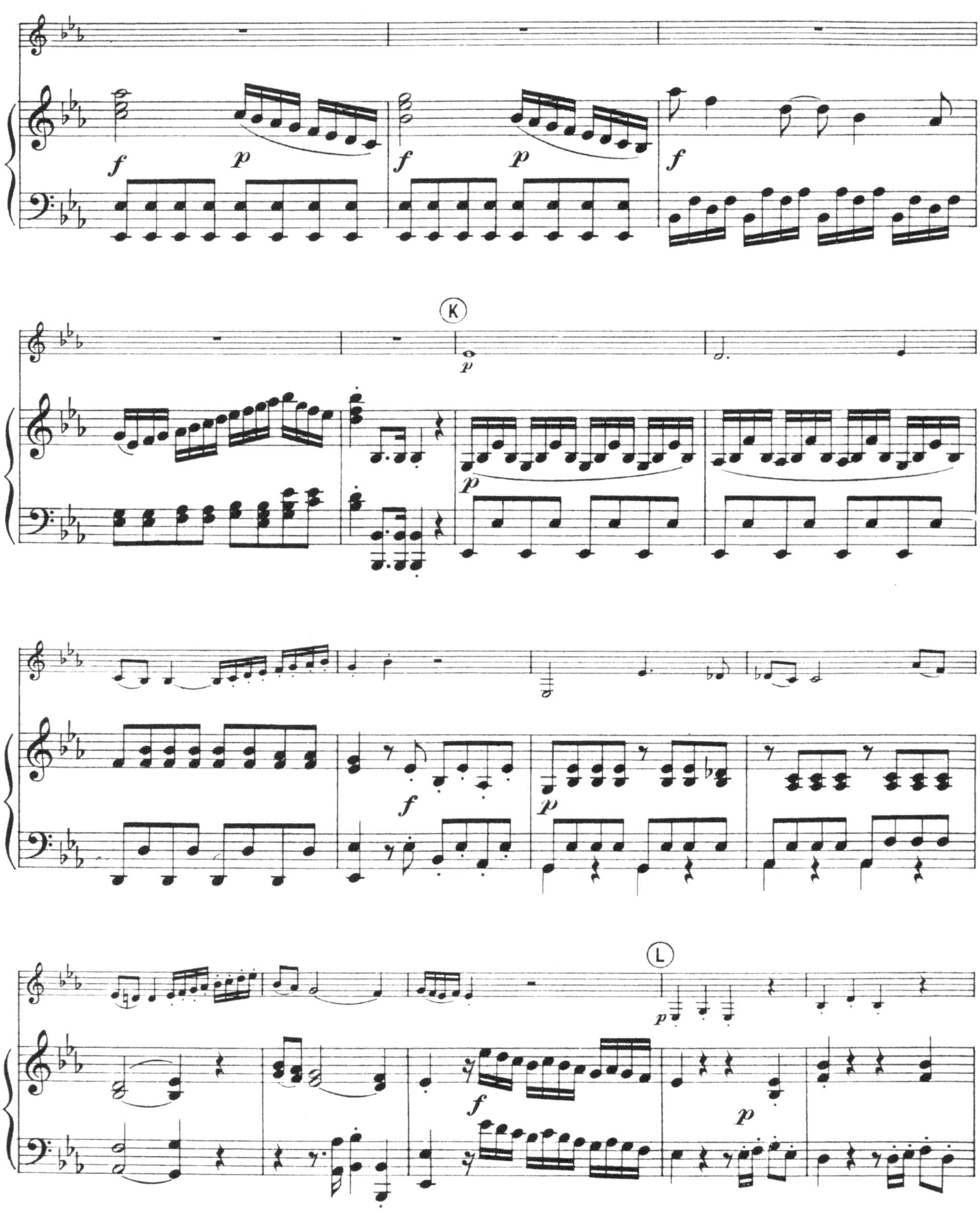
K
L

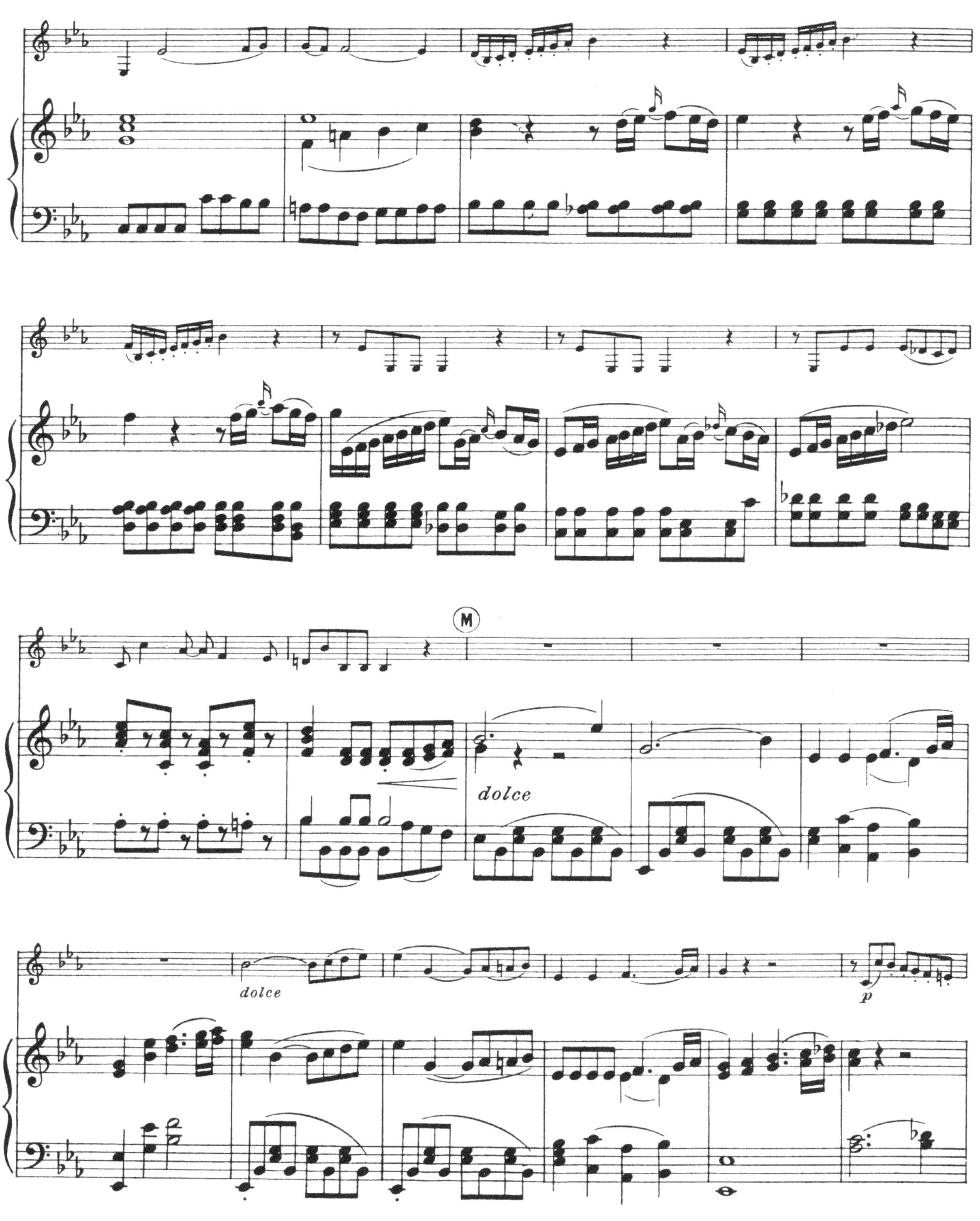
M
dolce
dolce
p

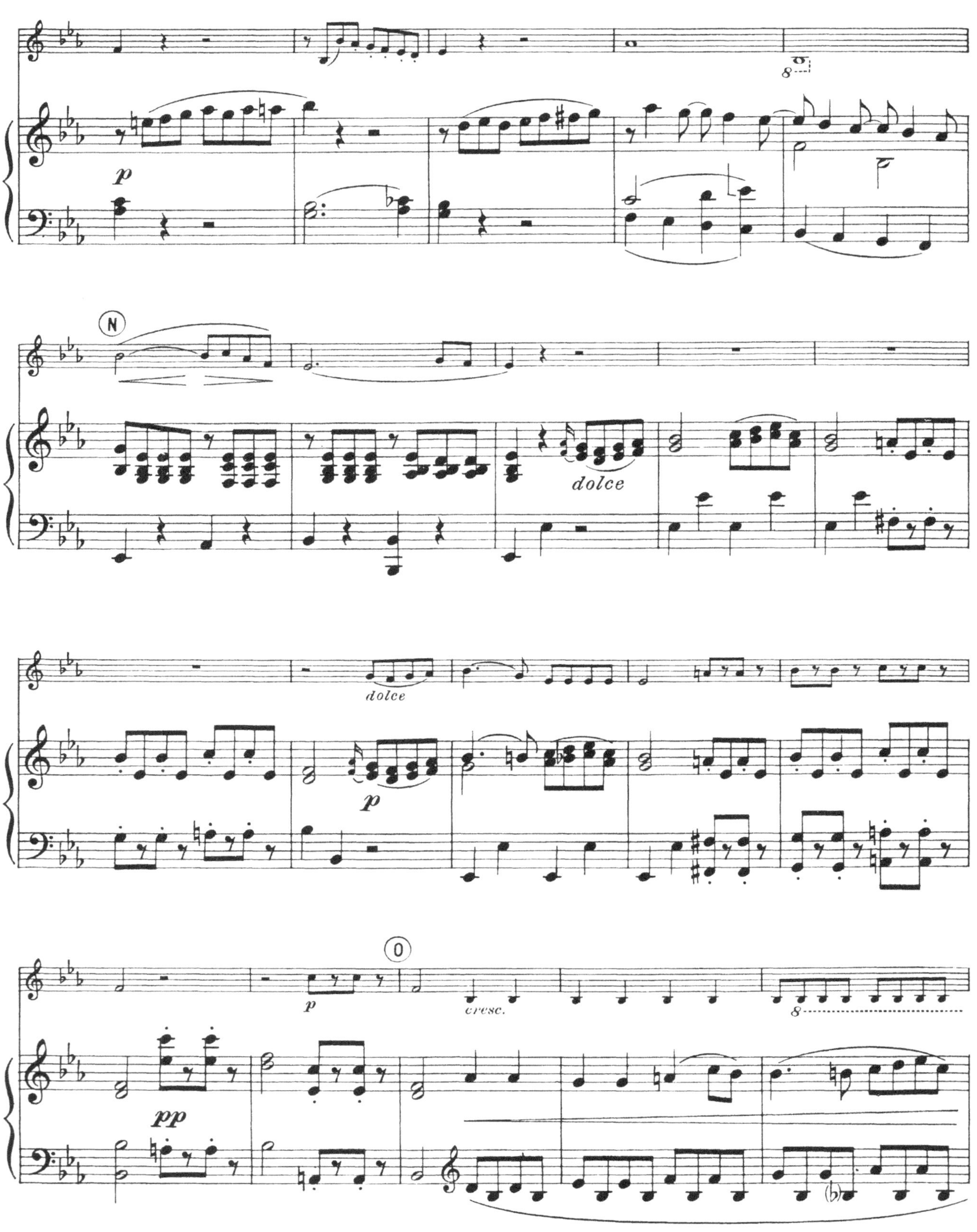
N
dolce
p
dolce
p
pp
O
p
cresc.

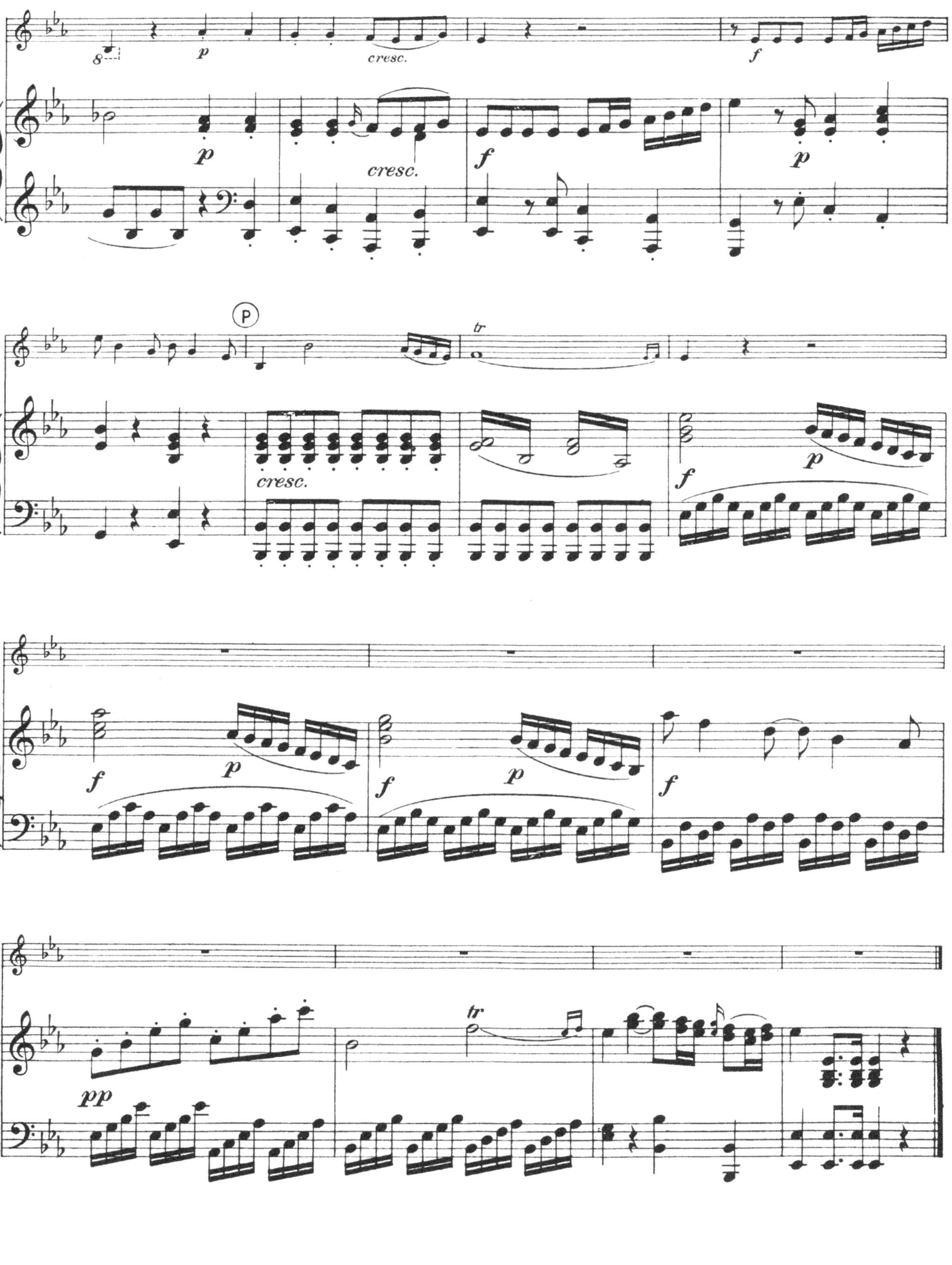
cresc.
P
tr
cresc.
tr

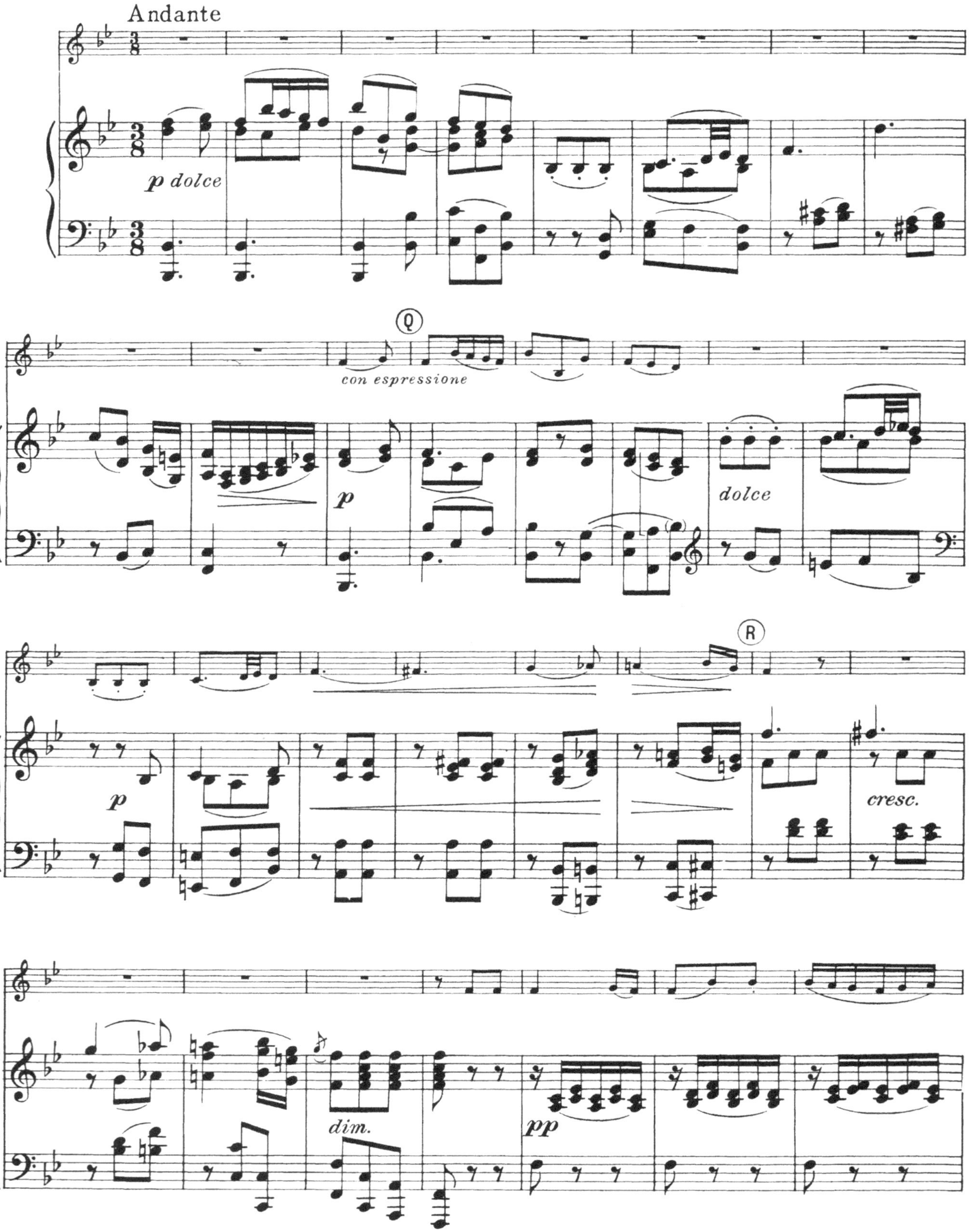
Andante
p dolce
Q
con espressione
p
dolce
R
p
cresc.
dim.
pp

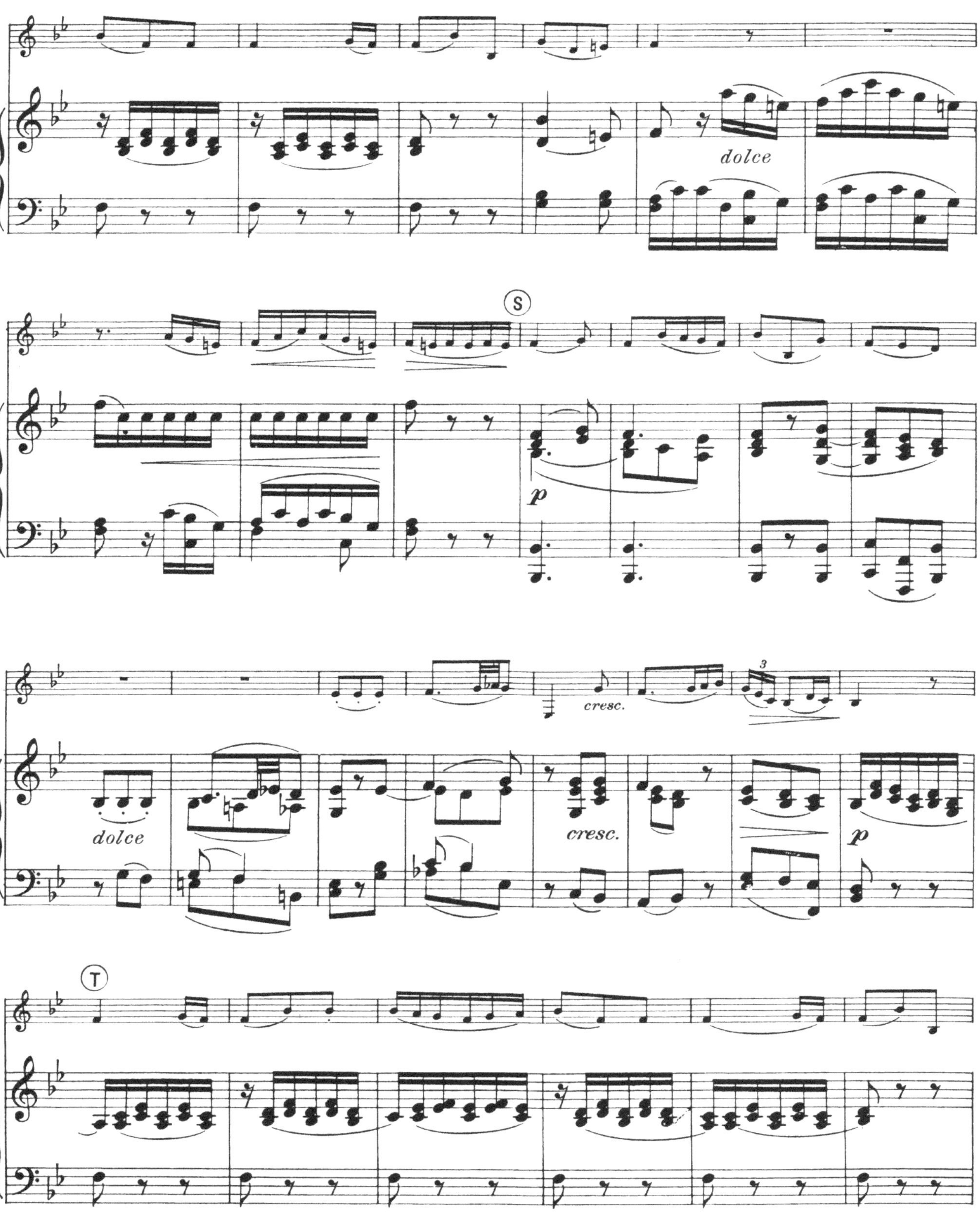
dolce
S
p
dolce
cresc.
cresc.
3
p
T

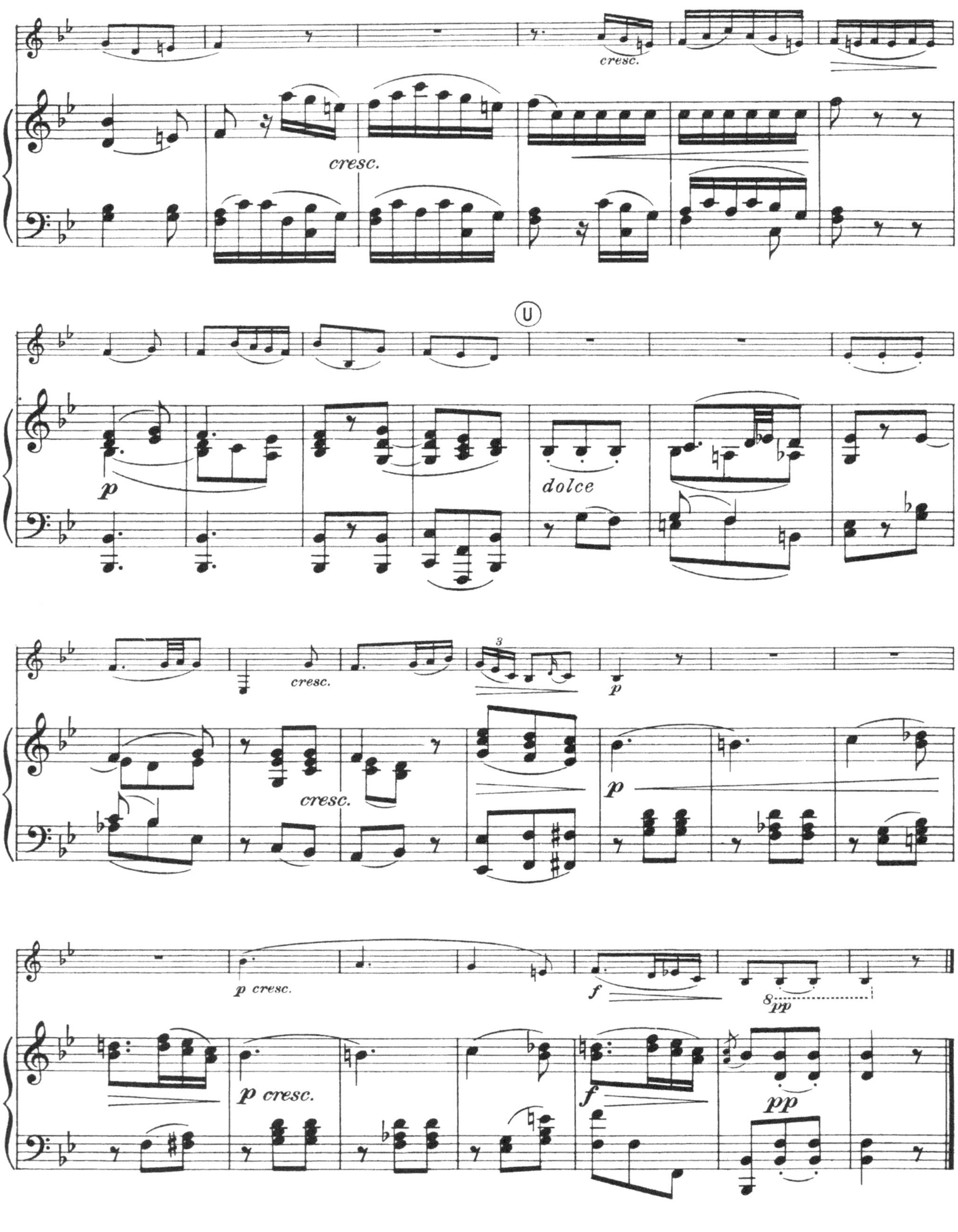
cresc.
cresc.
U
p
dolce
cresc.
cresc.
3
p
p
p cresc.
p cresc.
f
f
8
pp
pp

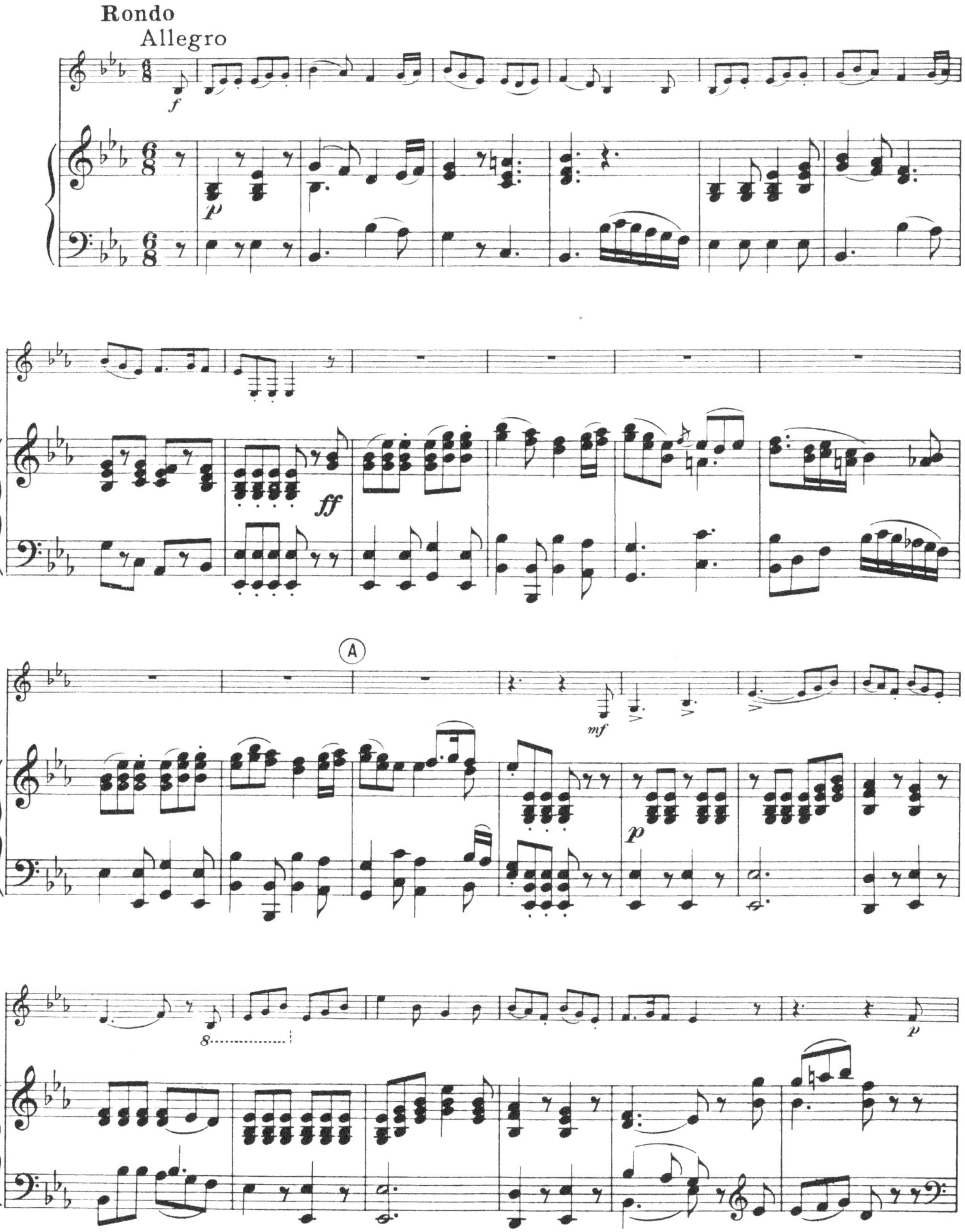
Rondo
Allegro
A

B
dim.
dim.
fp
p dim.
dim.
C
poco ritenuto e dim.
dolce
tr
tr
tr
f
p
poco ritenuto e dim.
Tempo I
p

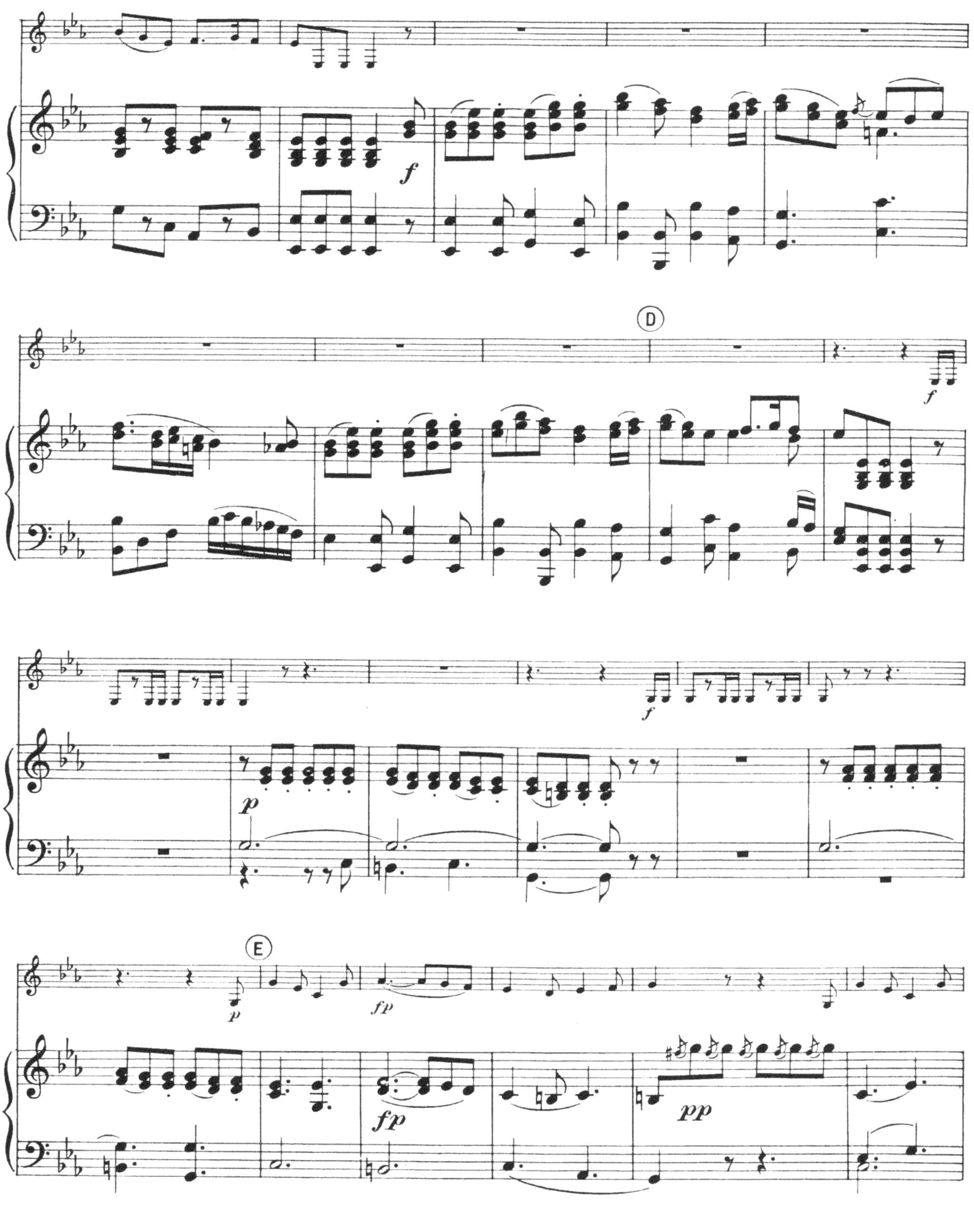
f
D
f
p
f
E
p
fp
fp
pp

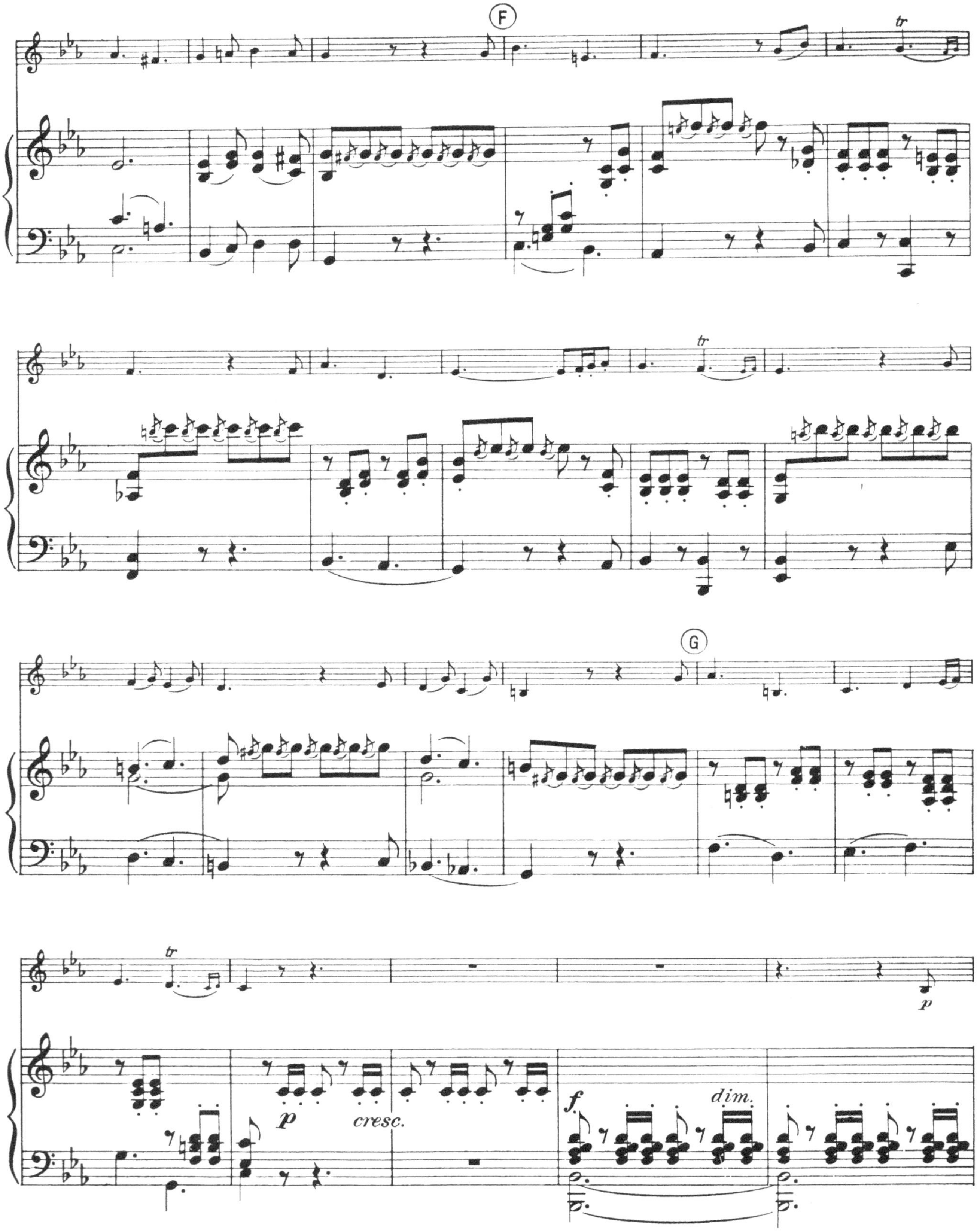
F
tr
tr
G
tr
p
cresc.
f
dim.
p

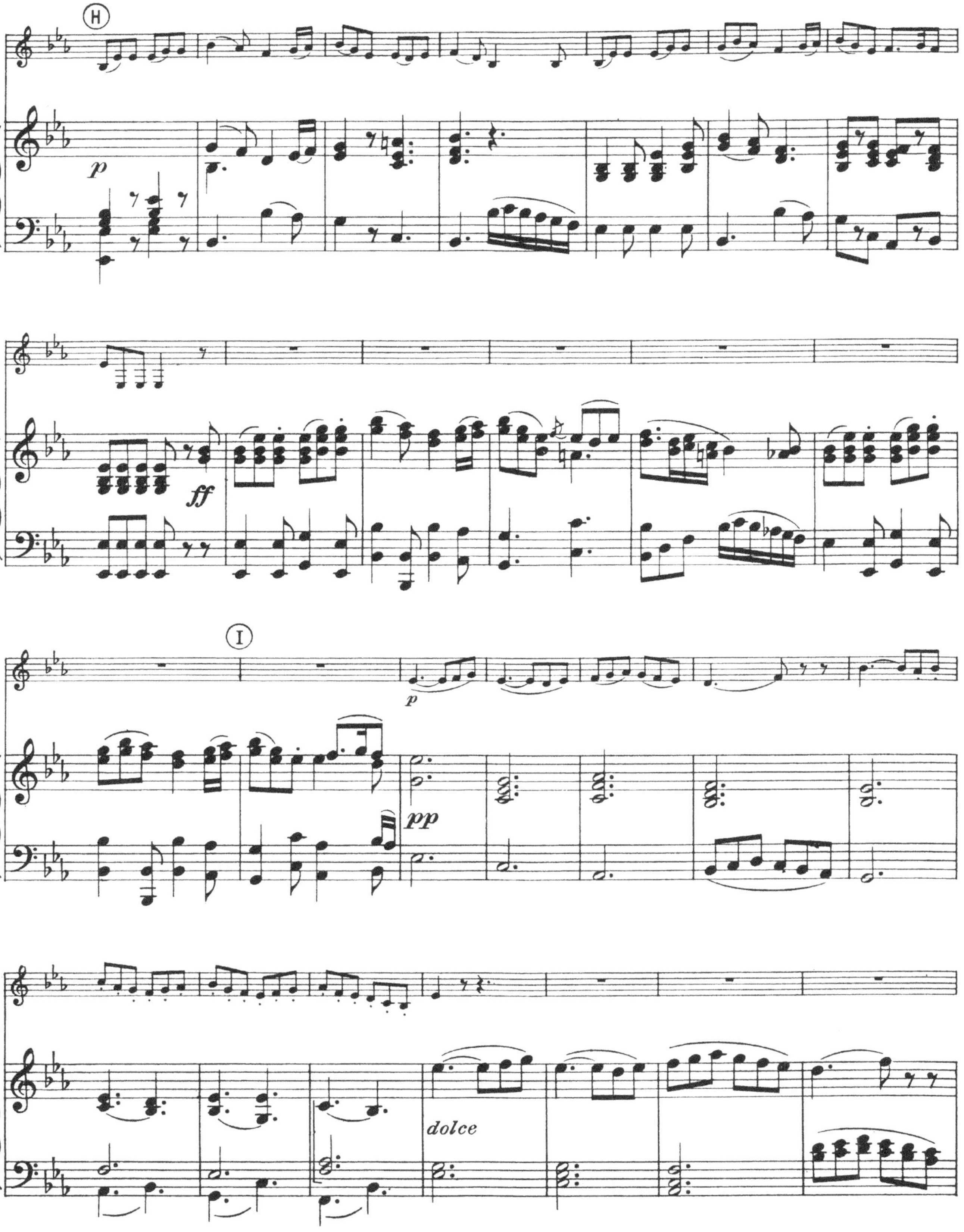
H
p
ff
I
p
pp
dolce

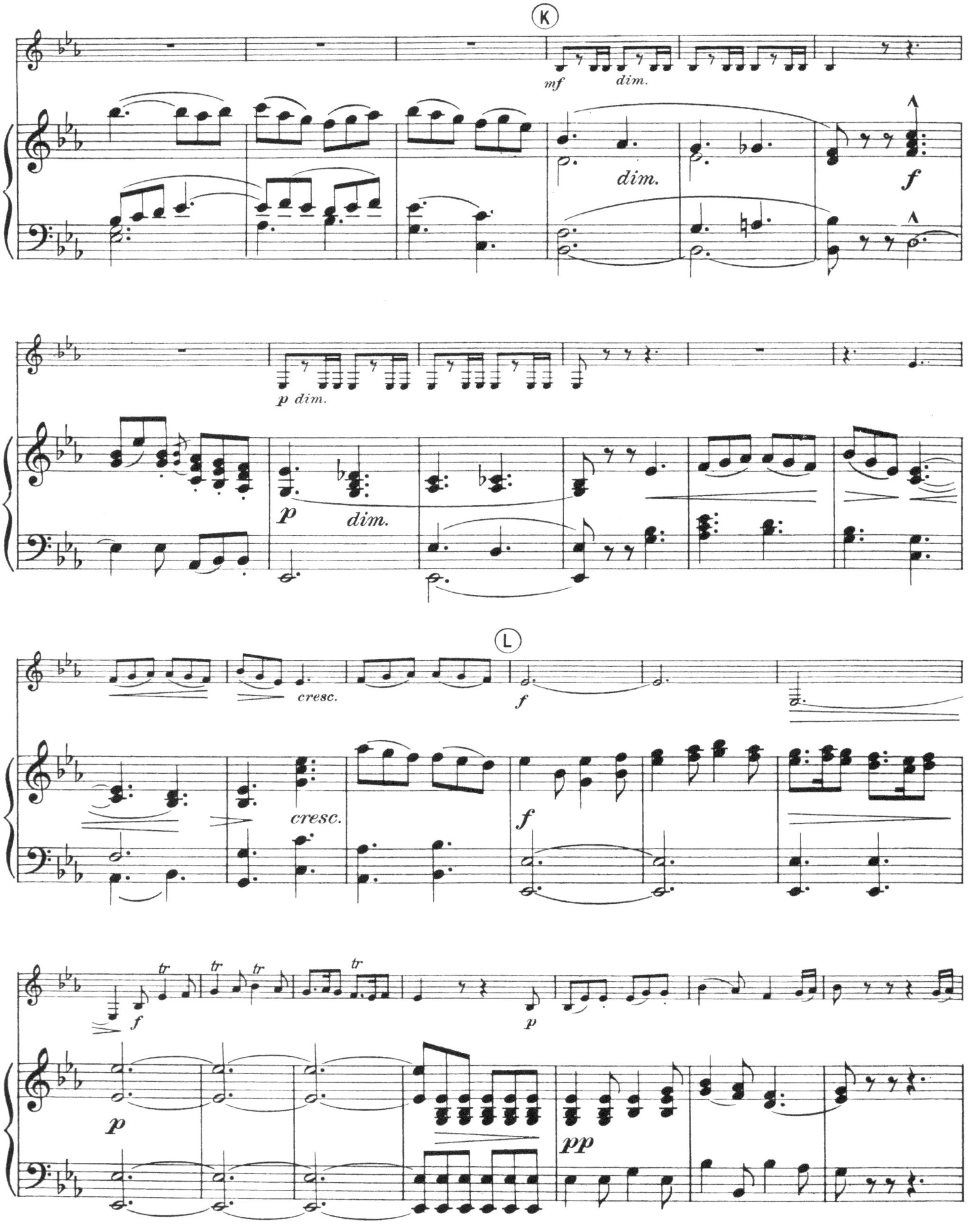
K
mf
dim.
dim.
f
p dim.
p
dim.
L
cresc.
cresc.
f
f
tr
f
p
p
pp

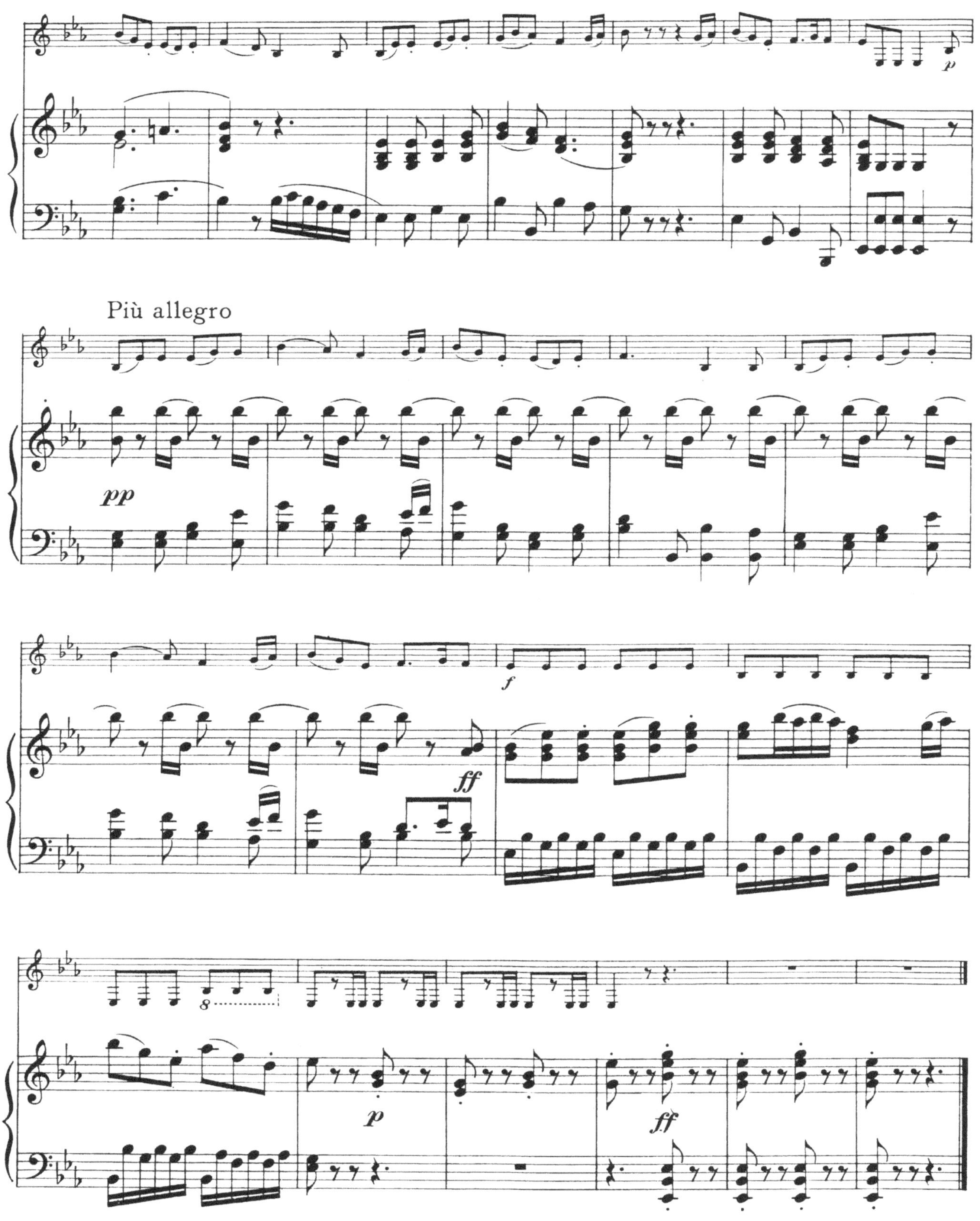
p
Più allegro
pp
f
ff
8
p
ff

Concerto No. 3 in E♭ Major

for Horn and Orchestra

[K.447]

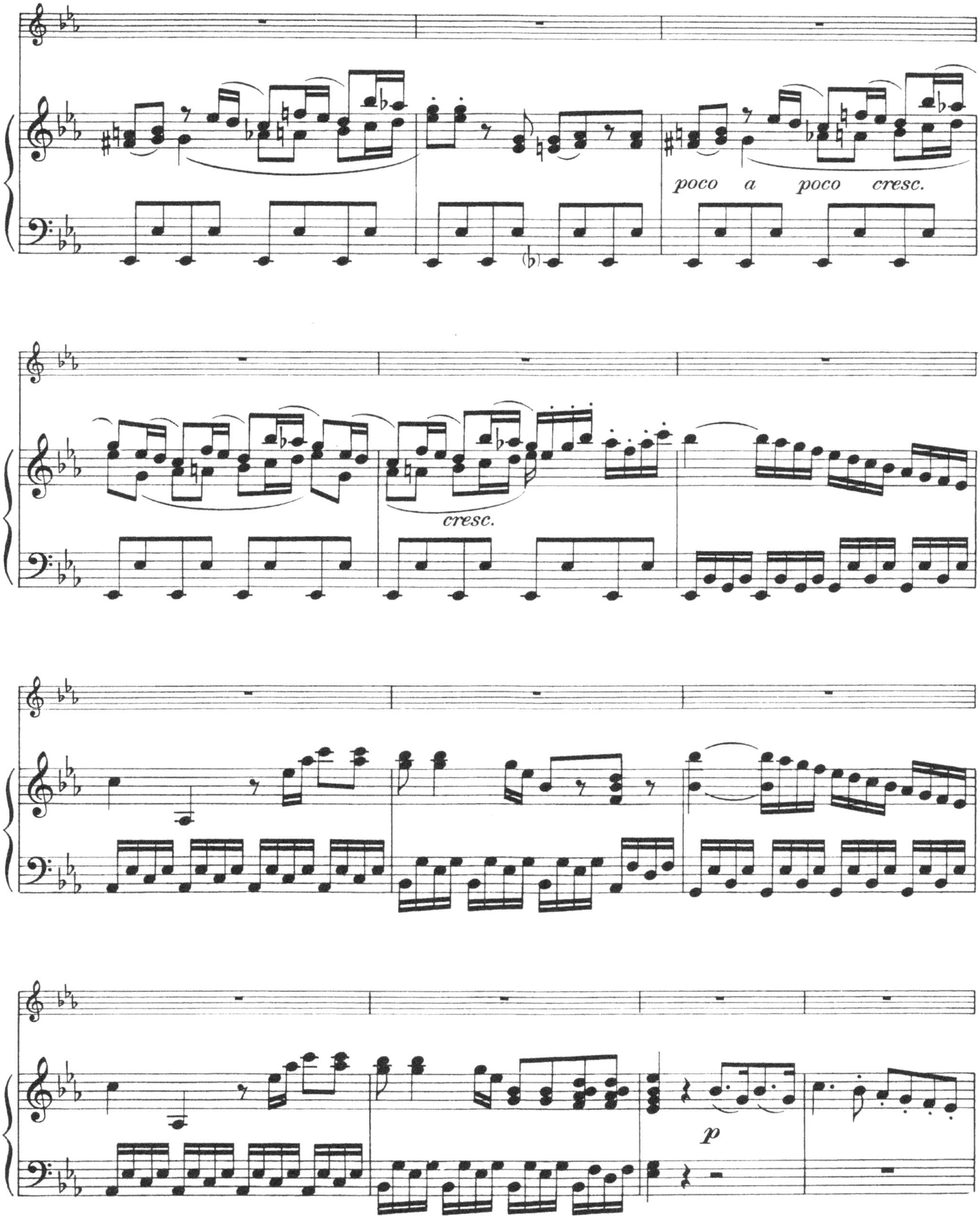
poco a poco cresc.
cresc.
p

Concerto No. 3 in E♭ Major

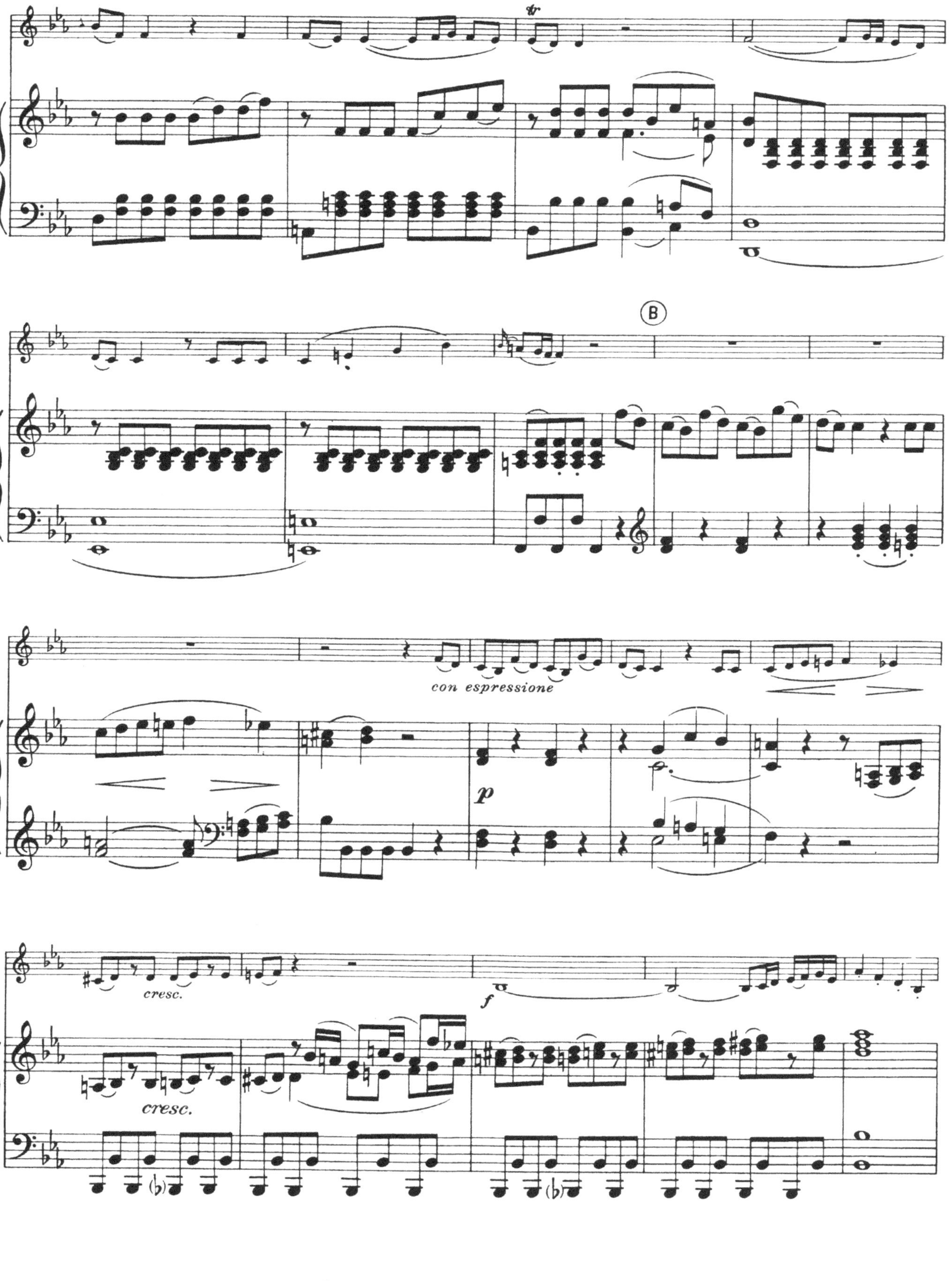
tr
B
con espressione
p
cresc.
cresc.
f

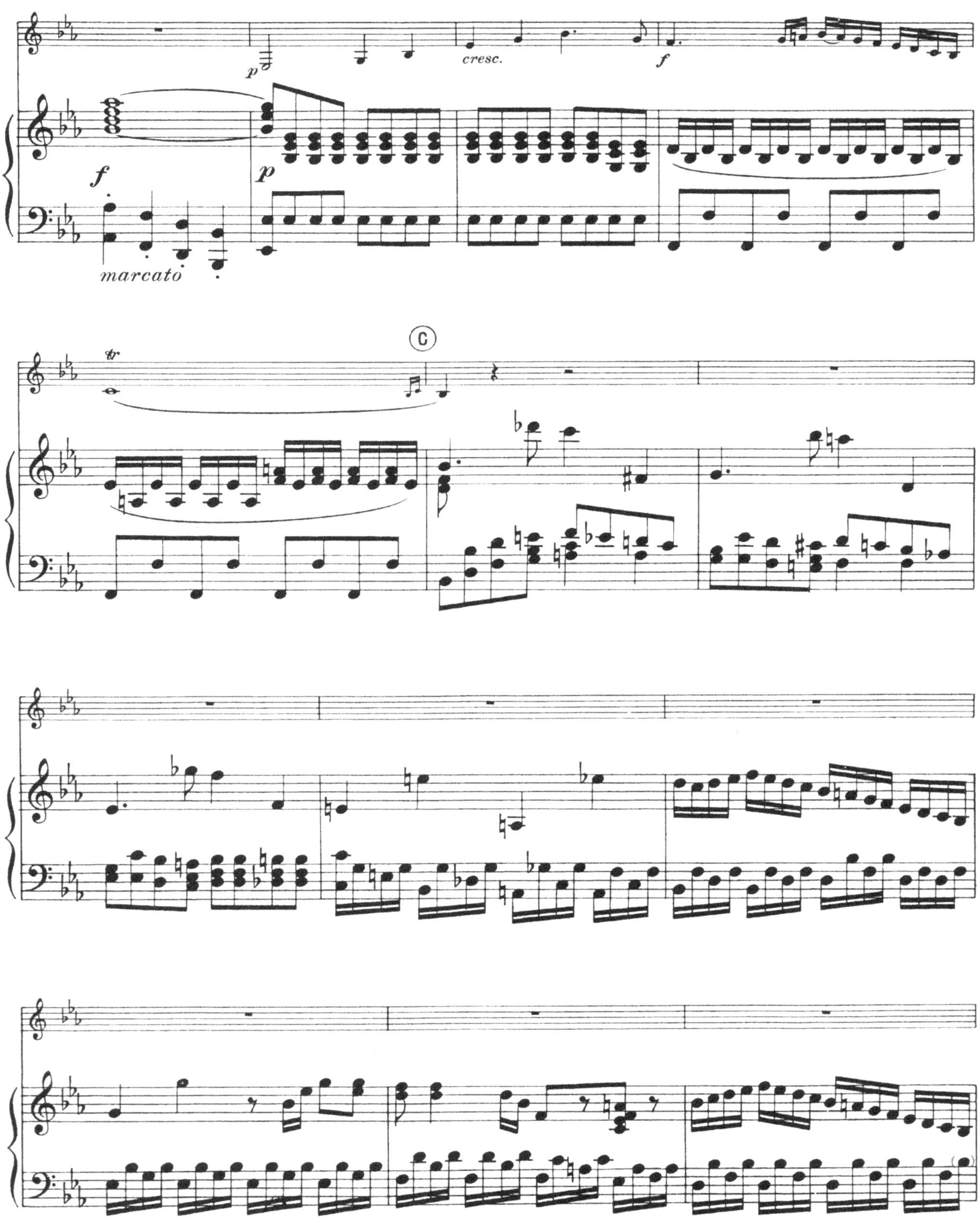

p
cresc.
f
f
p
marcato
tr
C

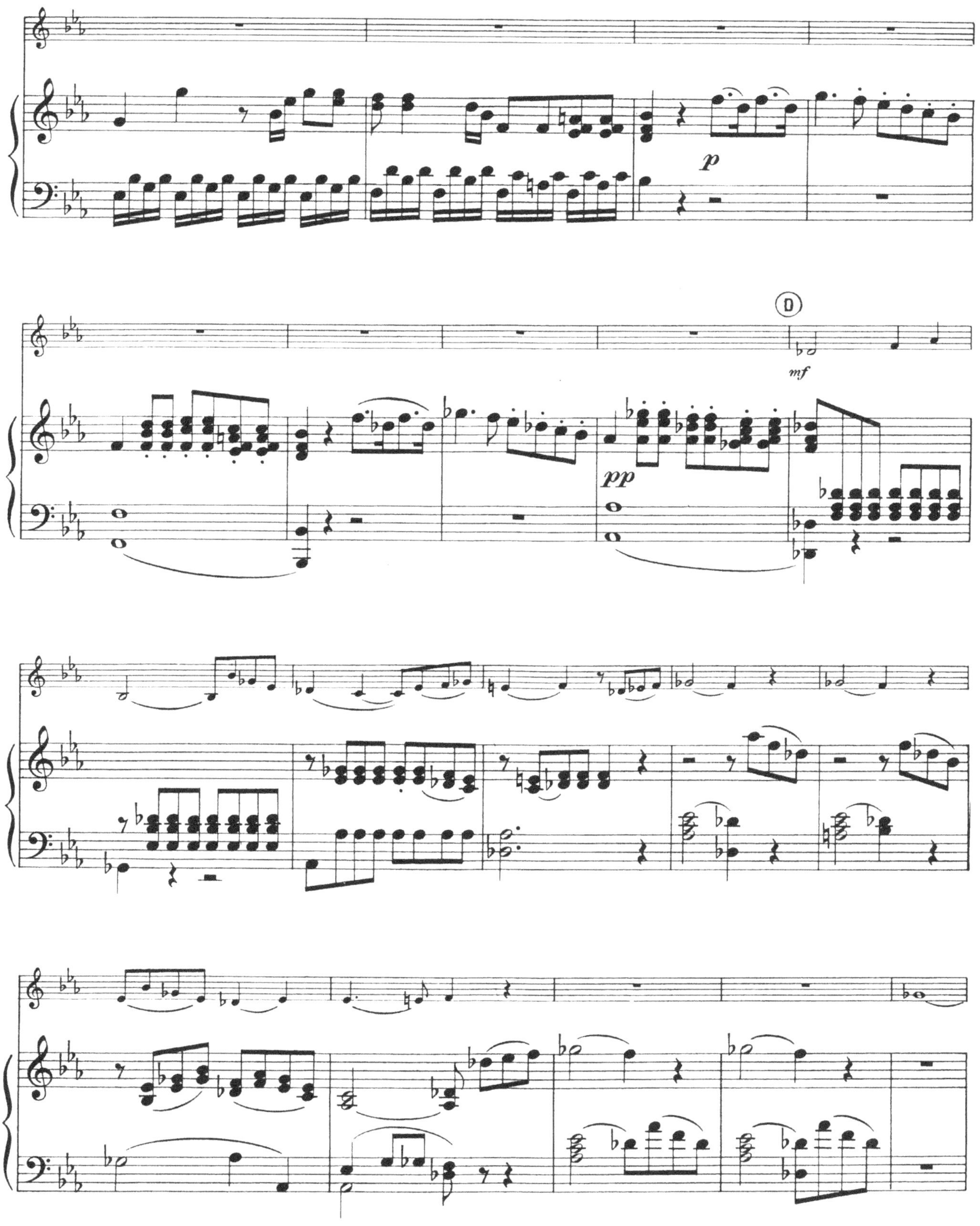
p
D
mf
pp

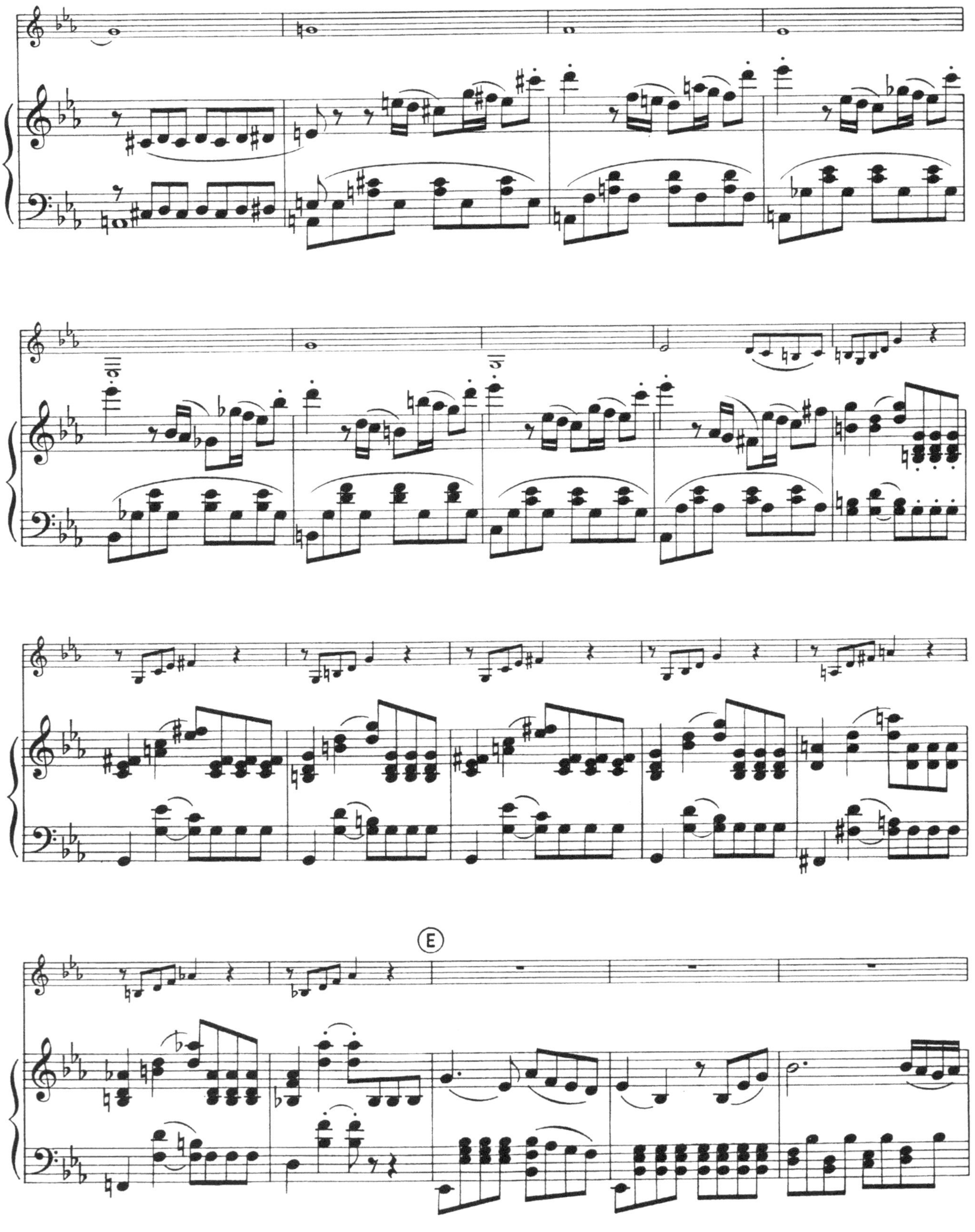
E

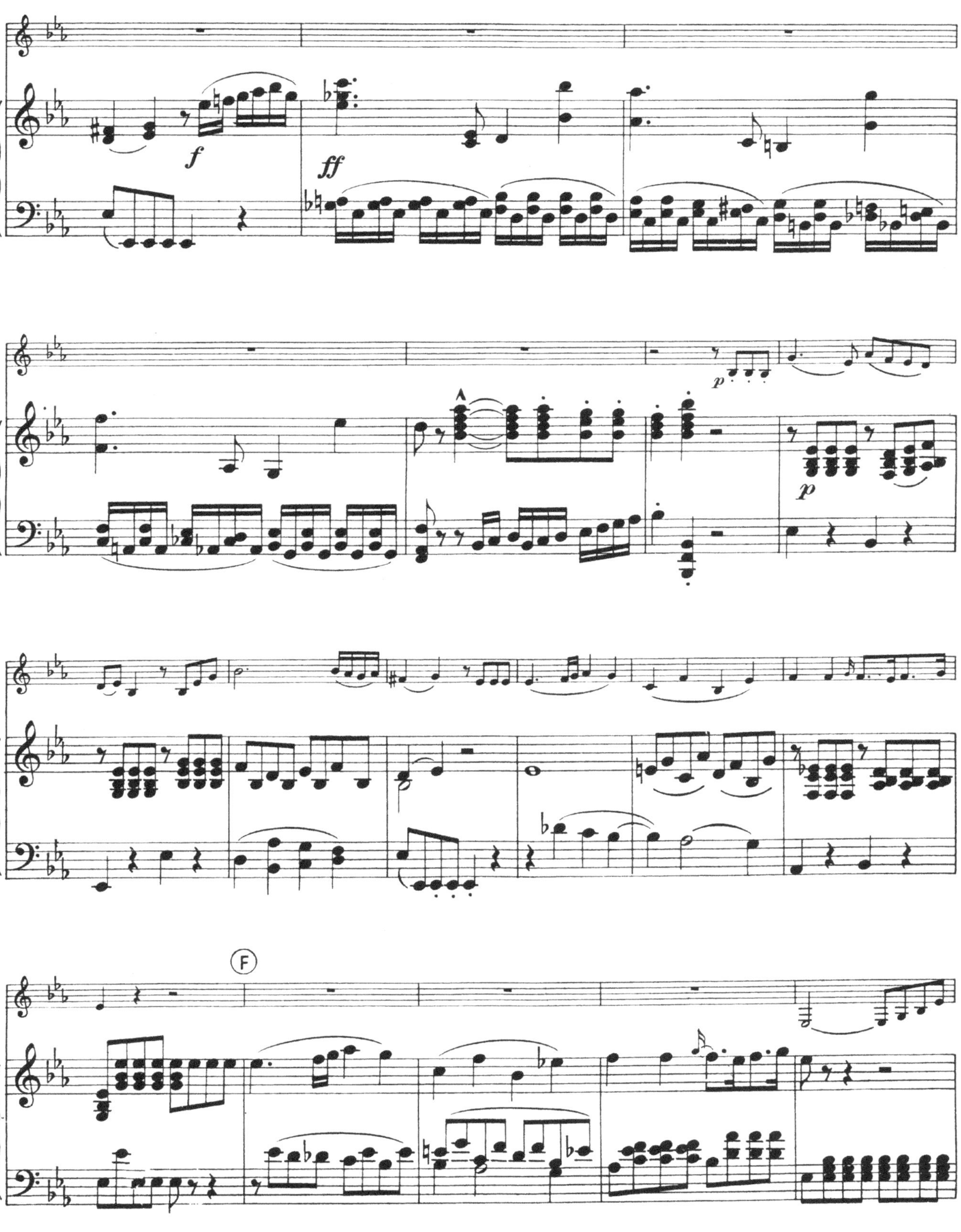
f
ff
p
p
F

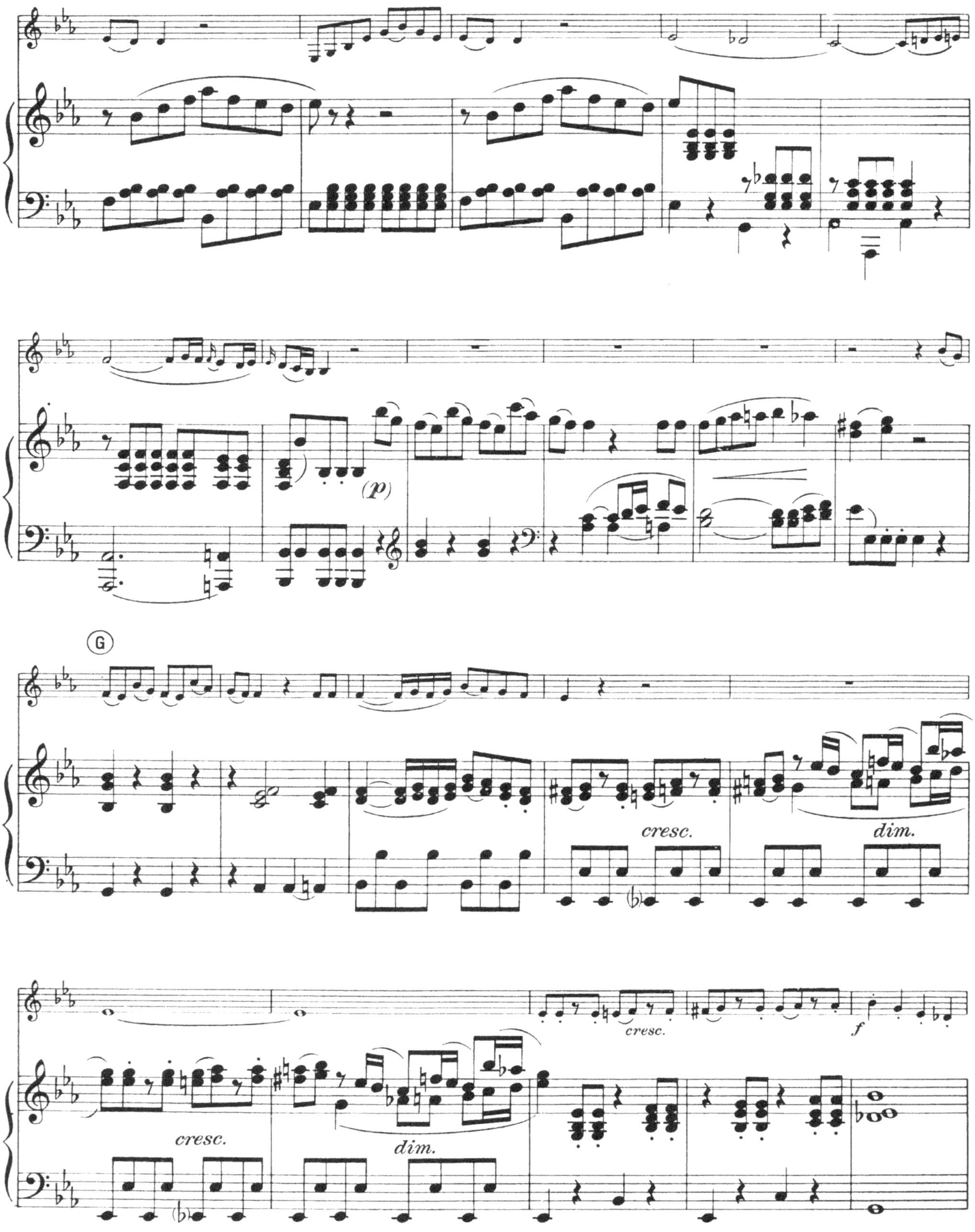
(p)
G
cresc.
dim.
cresc.
dim.
cresc.
f

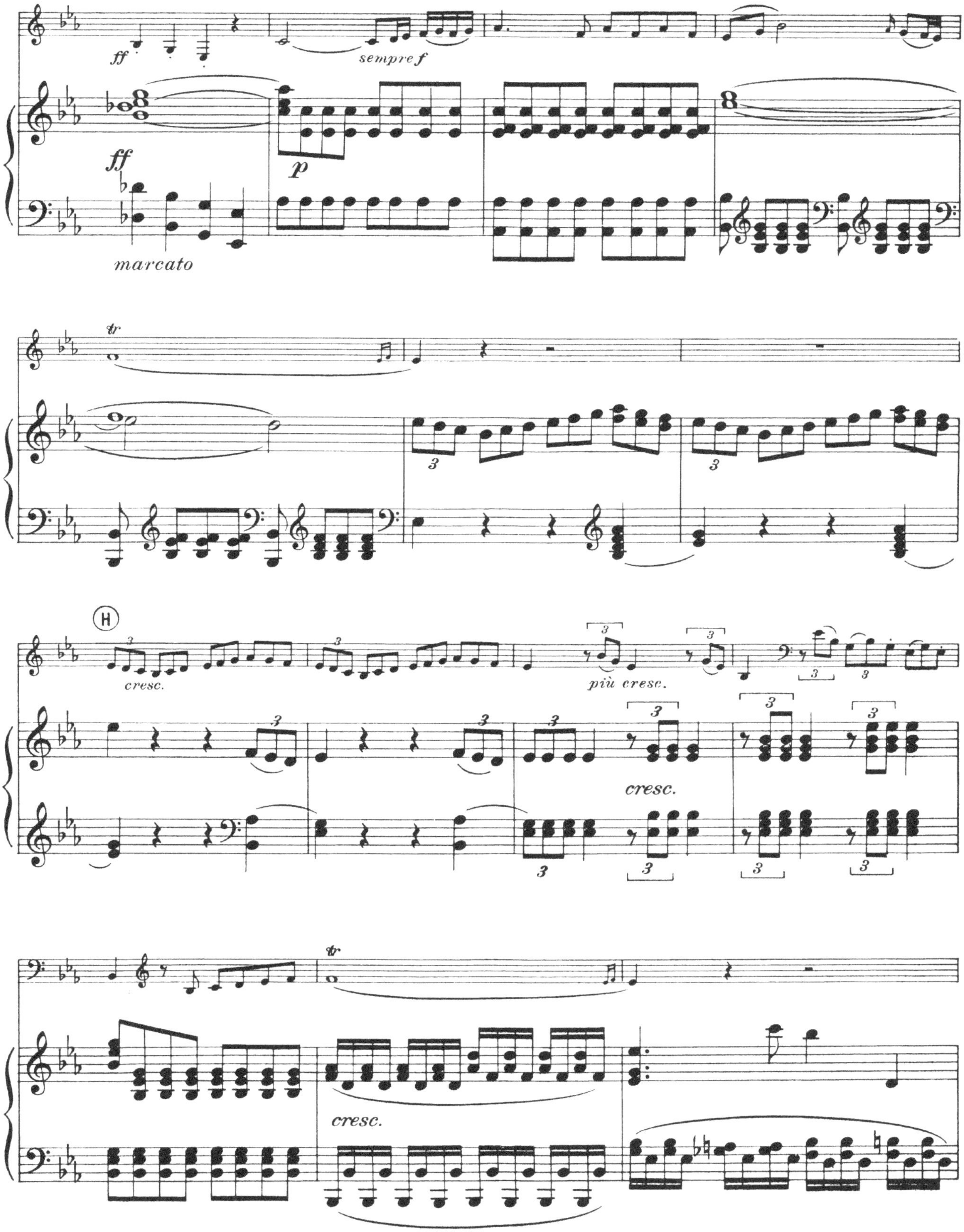
ff
sempre f
ff
p
marcato
tr
H
cresc.
più cresc.
cresc.
tr
cresc.

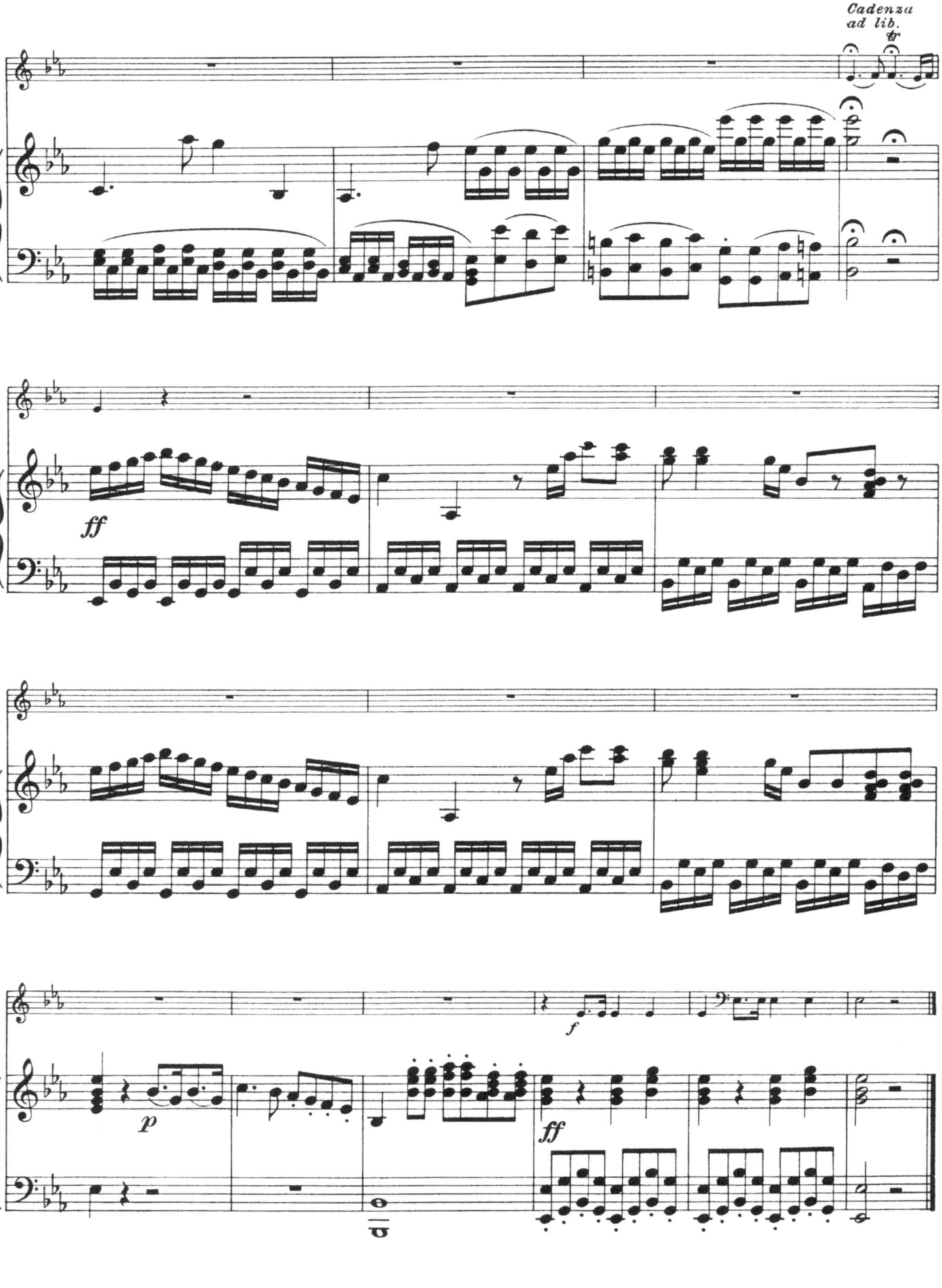
Cadenza
ad lib.
tr
ff
ff
p
ff
f

Romanze
Larghetto
p con molto espressione
pp
A
f
f
cresc.
f
p
mf
f

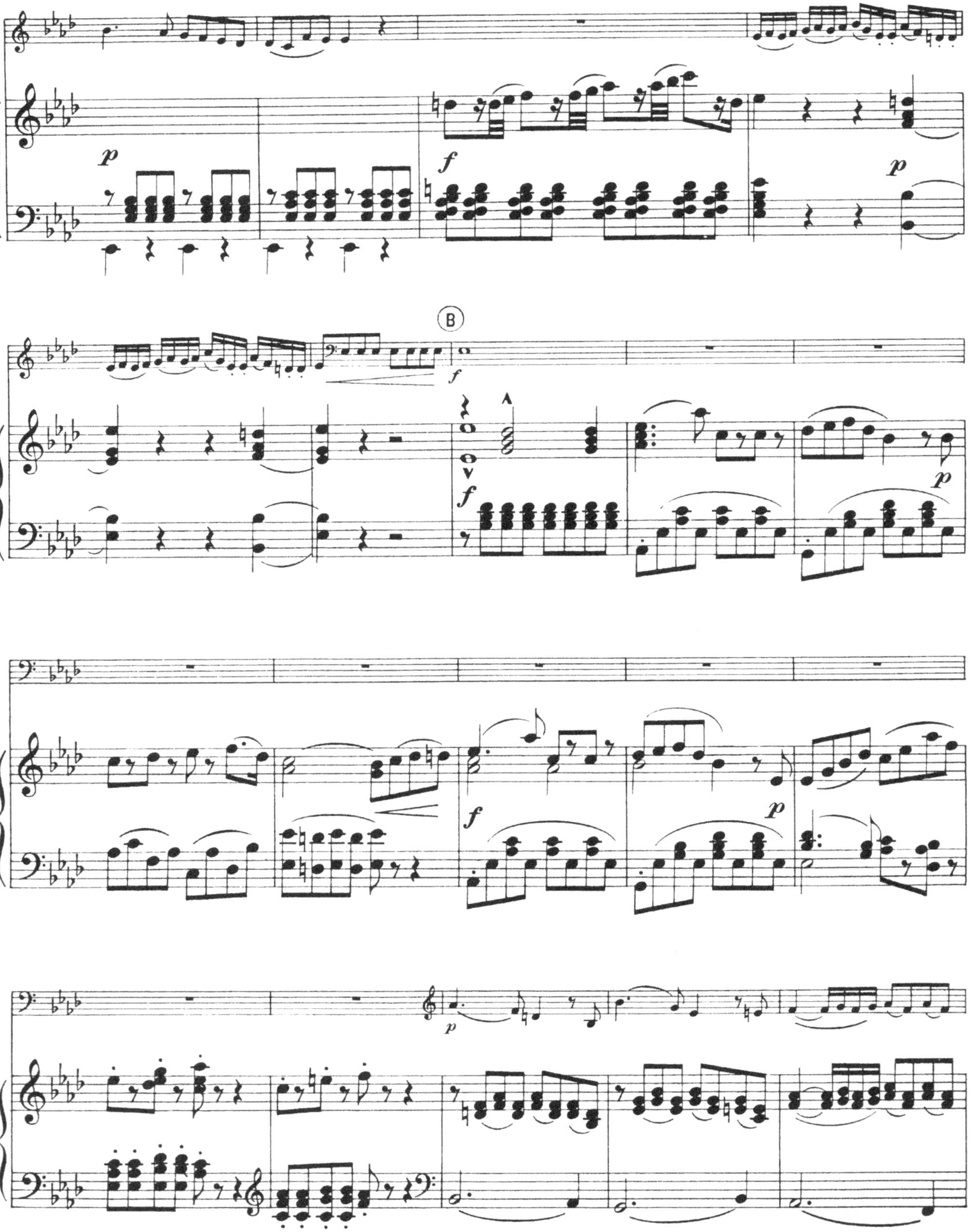
B
p
f

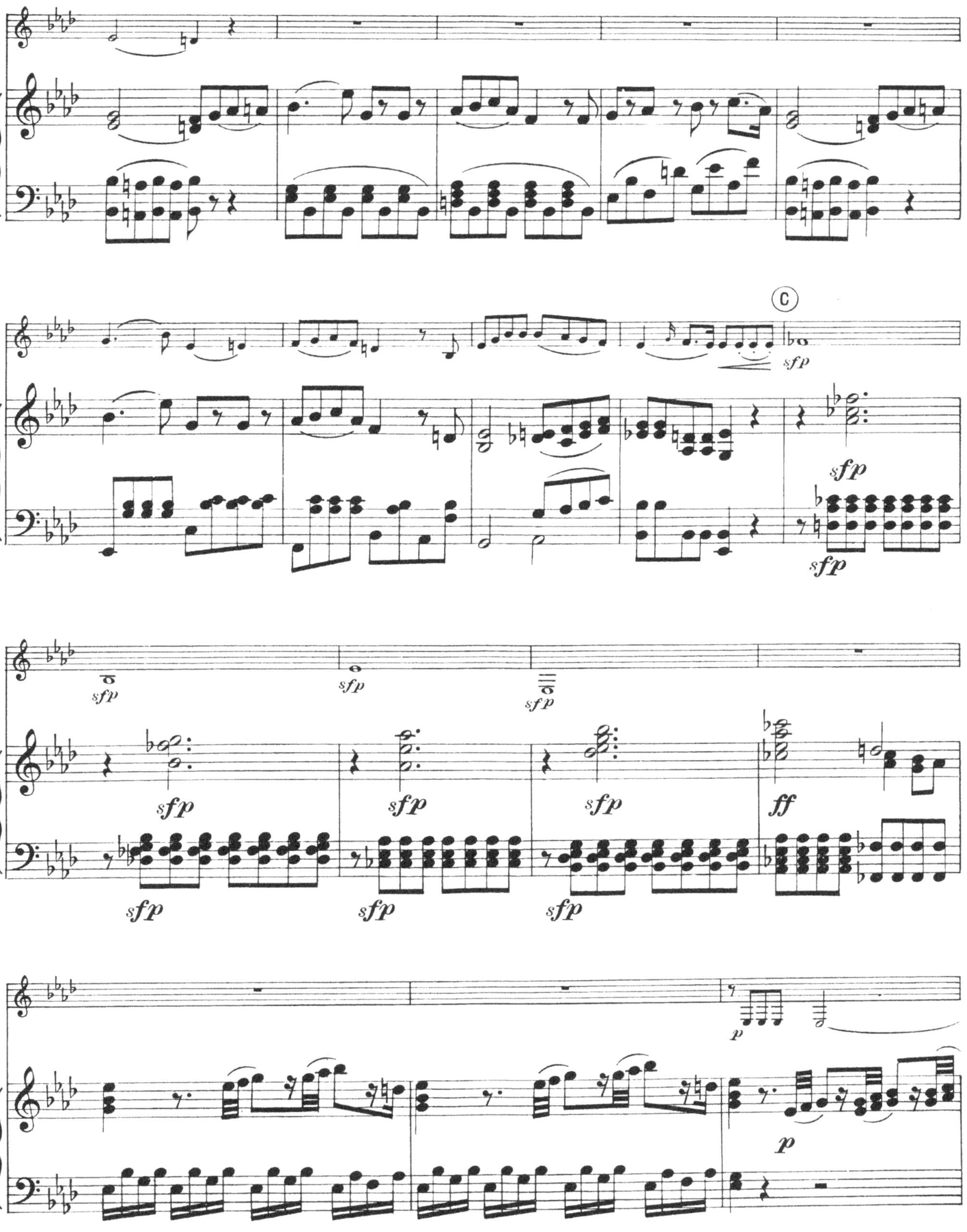
C
sfp
ff
p

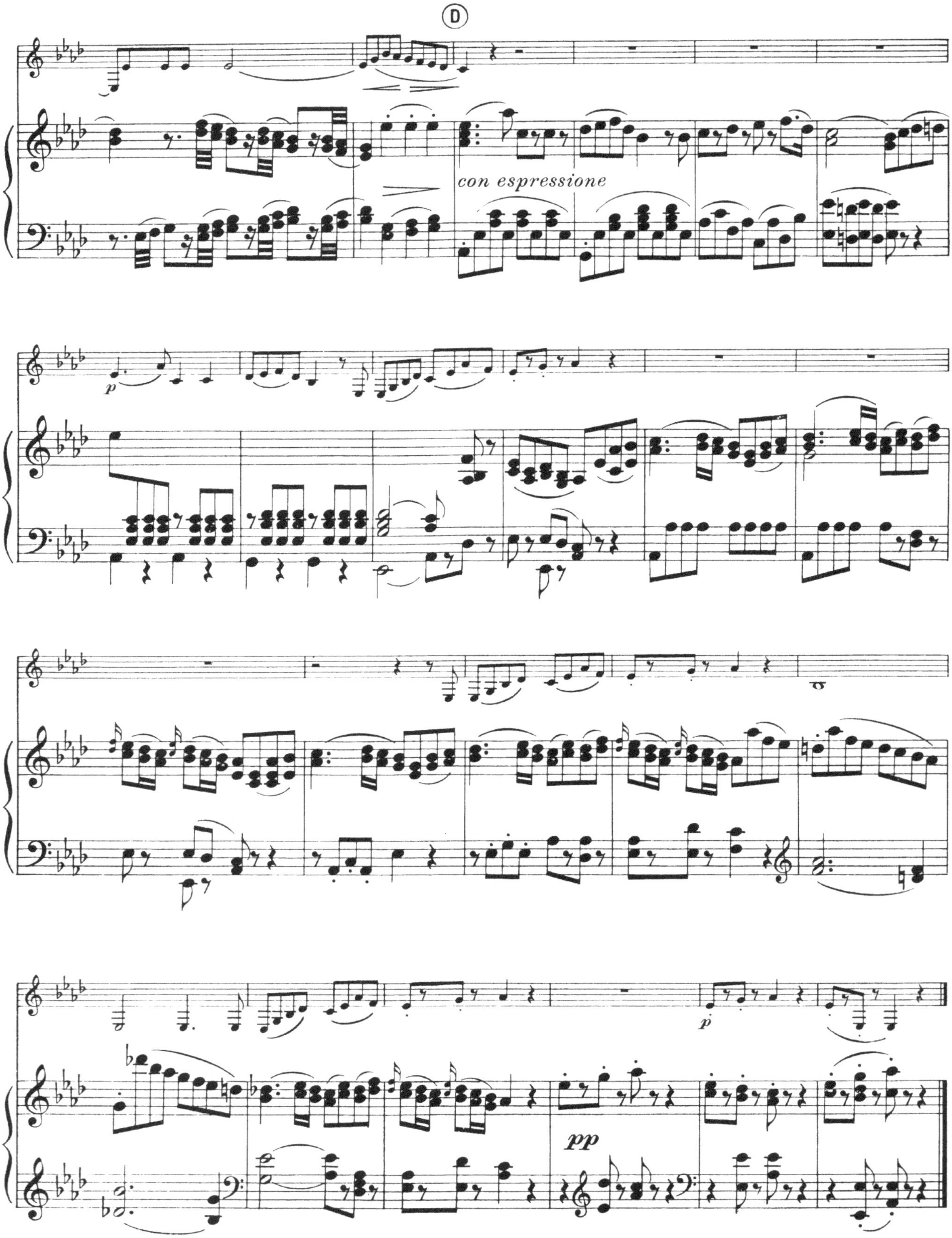
D
con espressione
p
p
pp
p

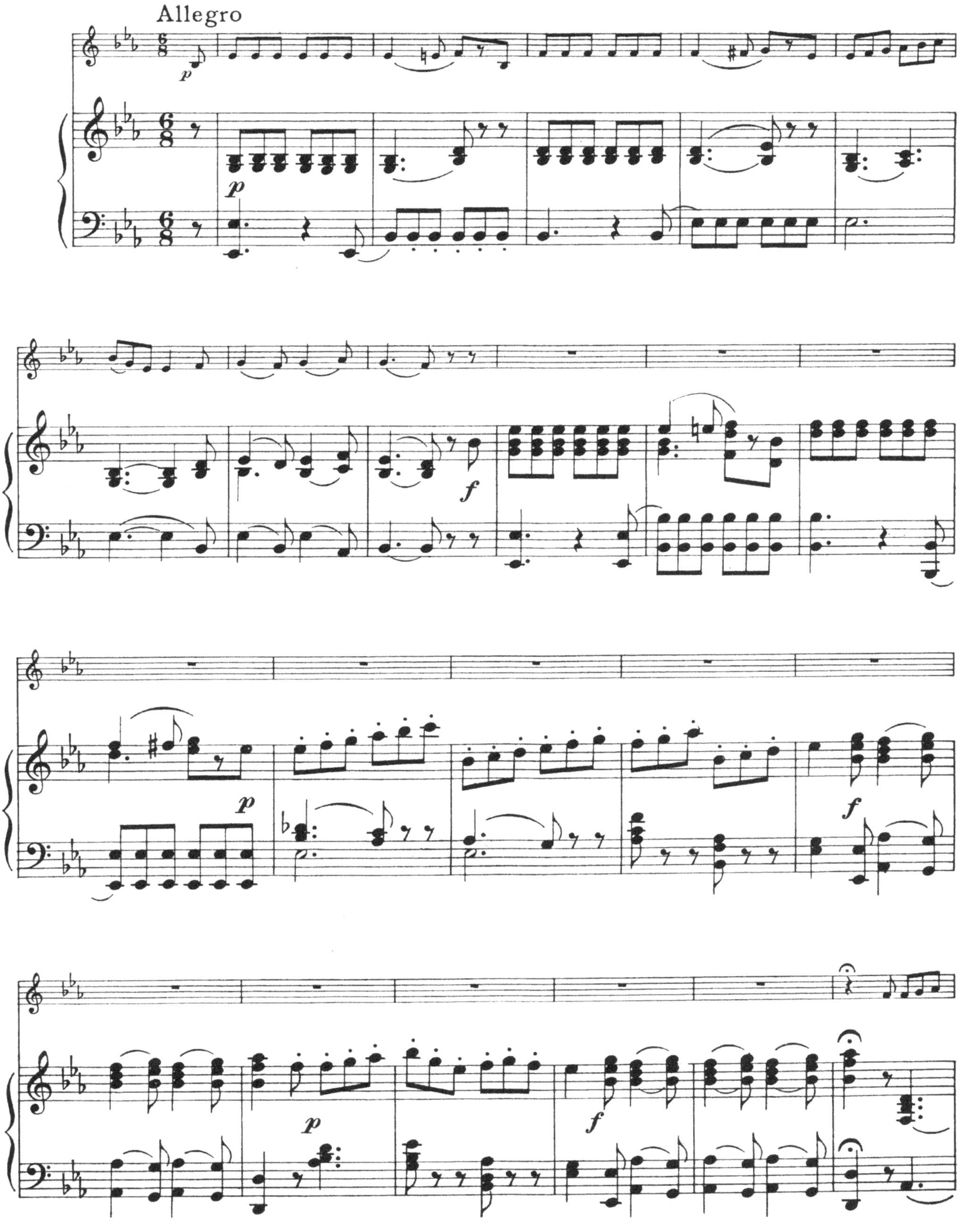
Allegro
p
p
f
p
f
p
f

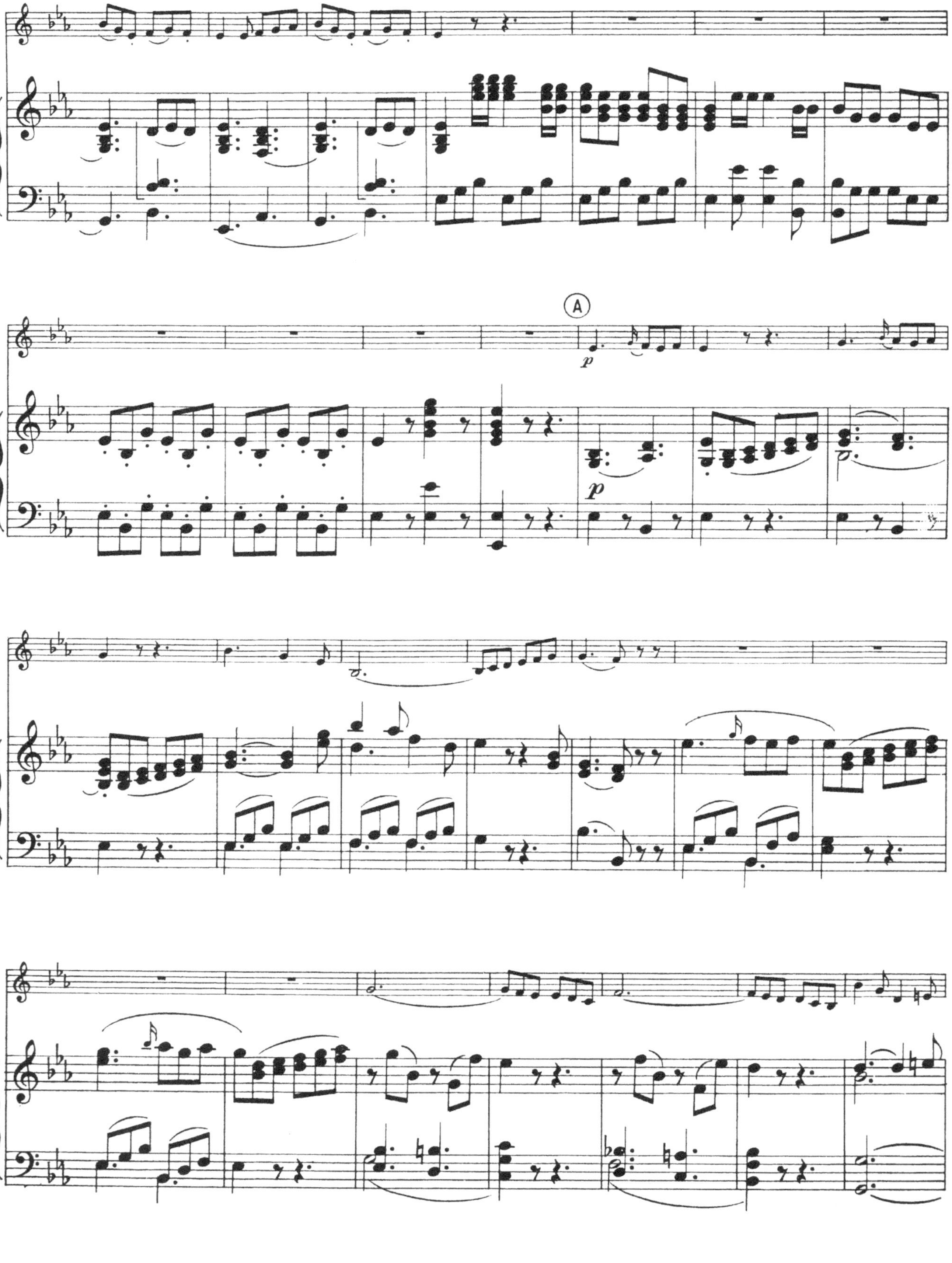
A
p
p

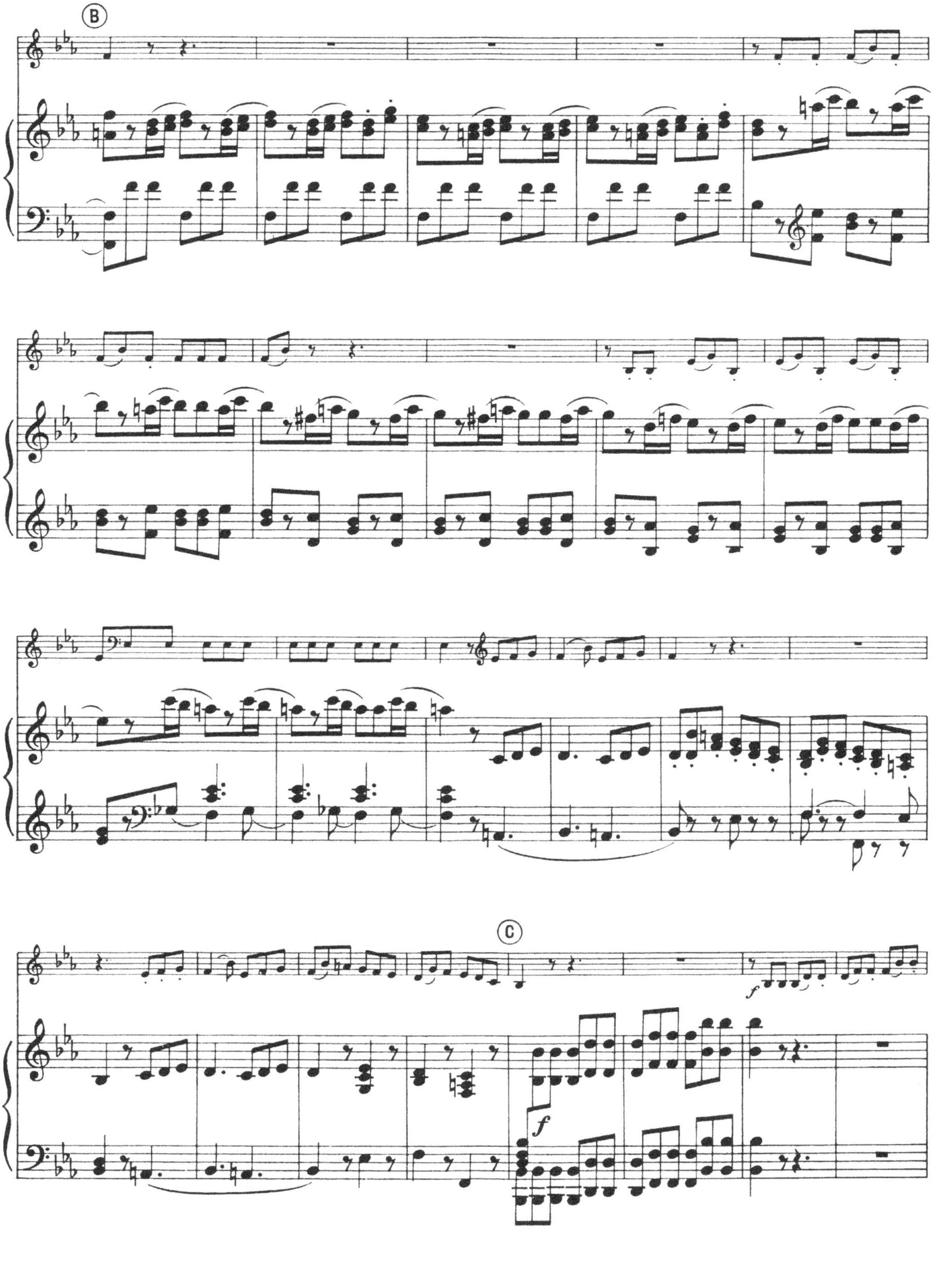
B
C
f
f

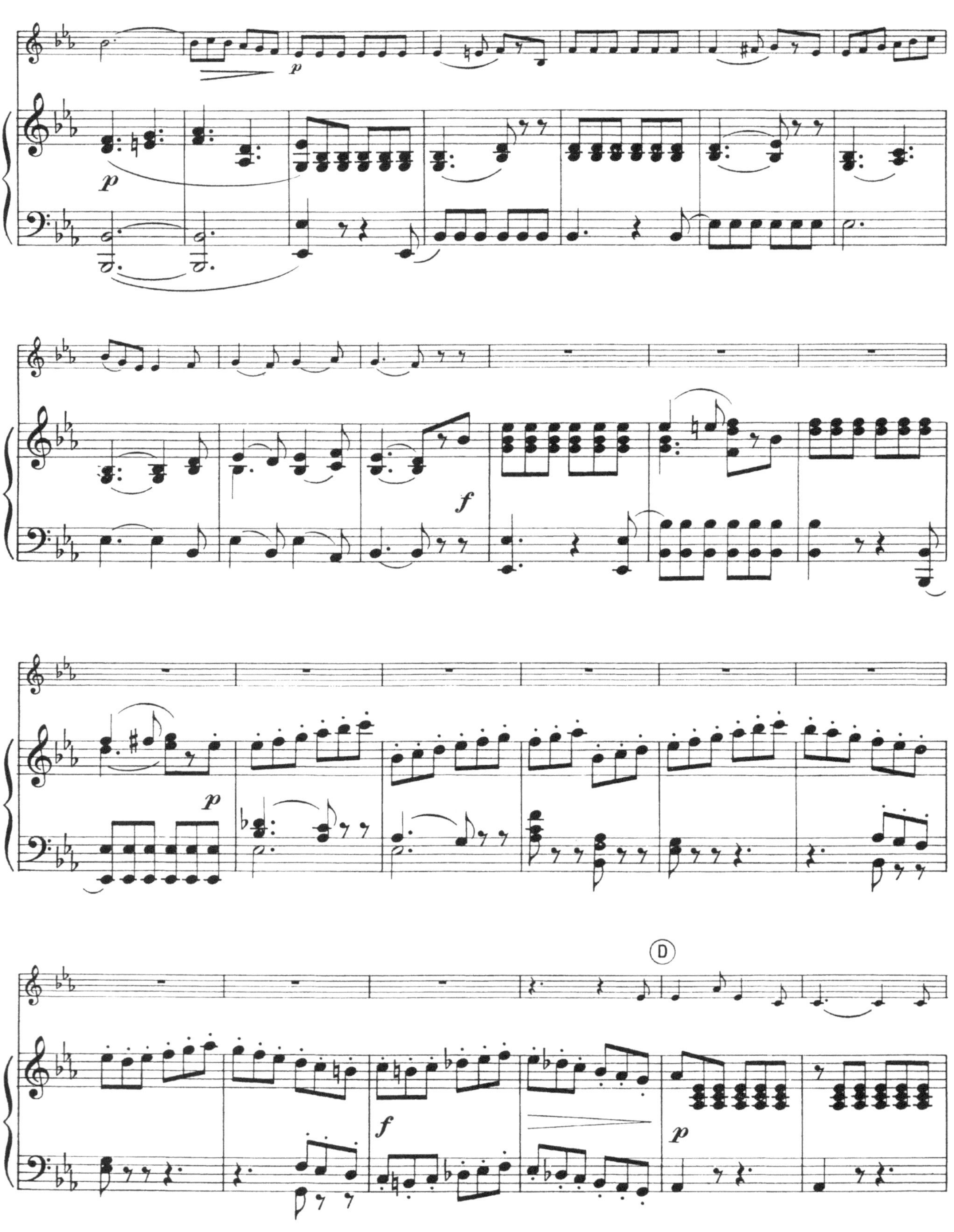
D

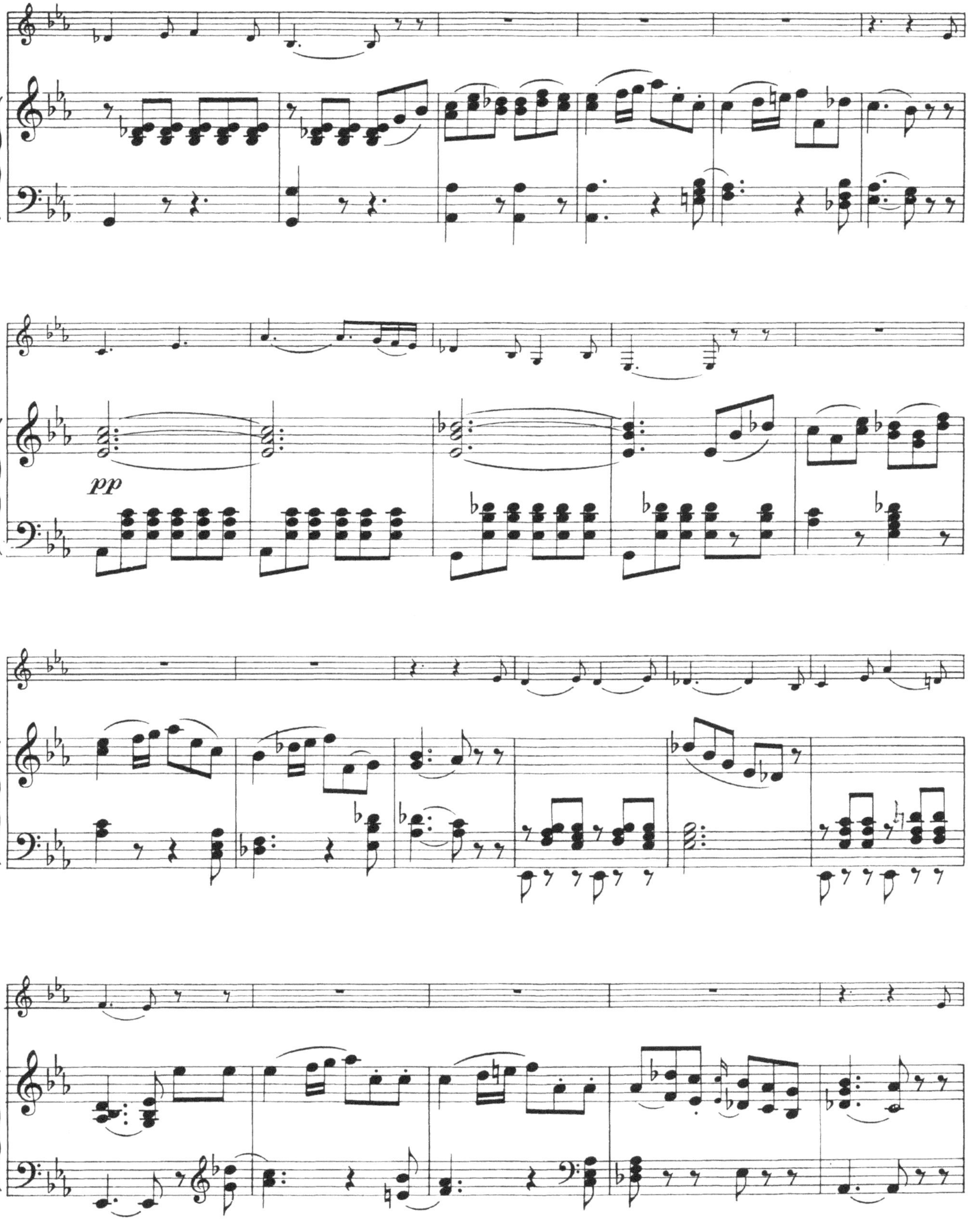
pp

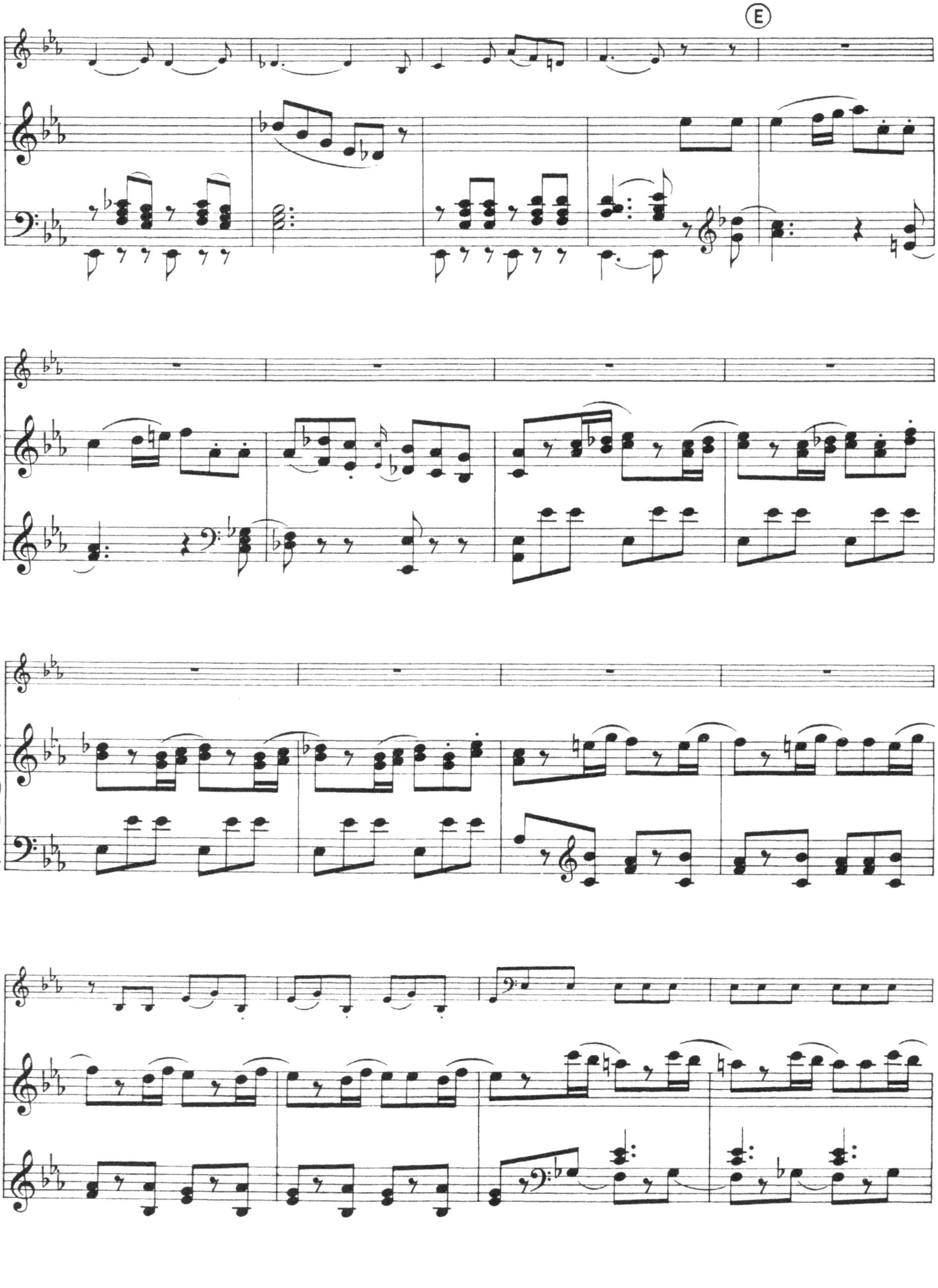
E

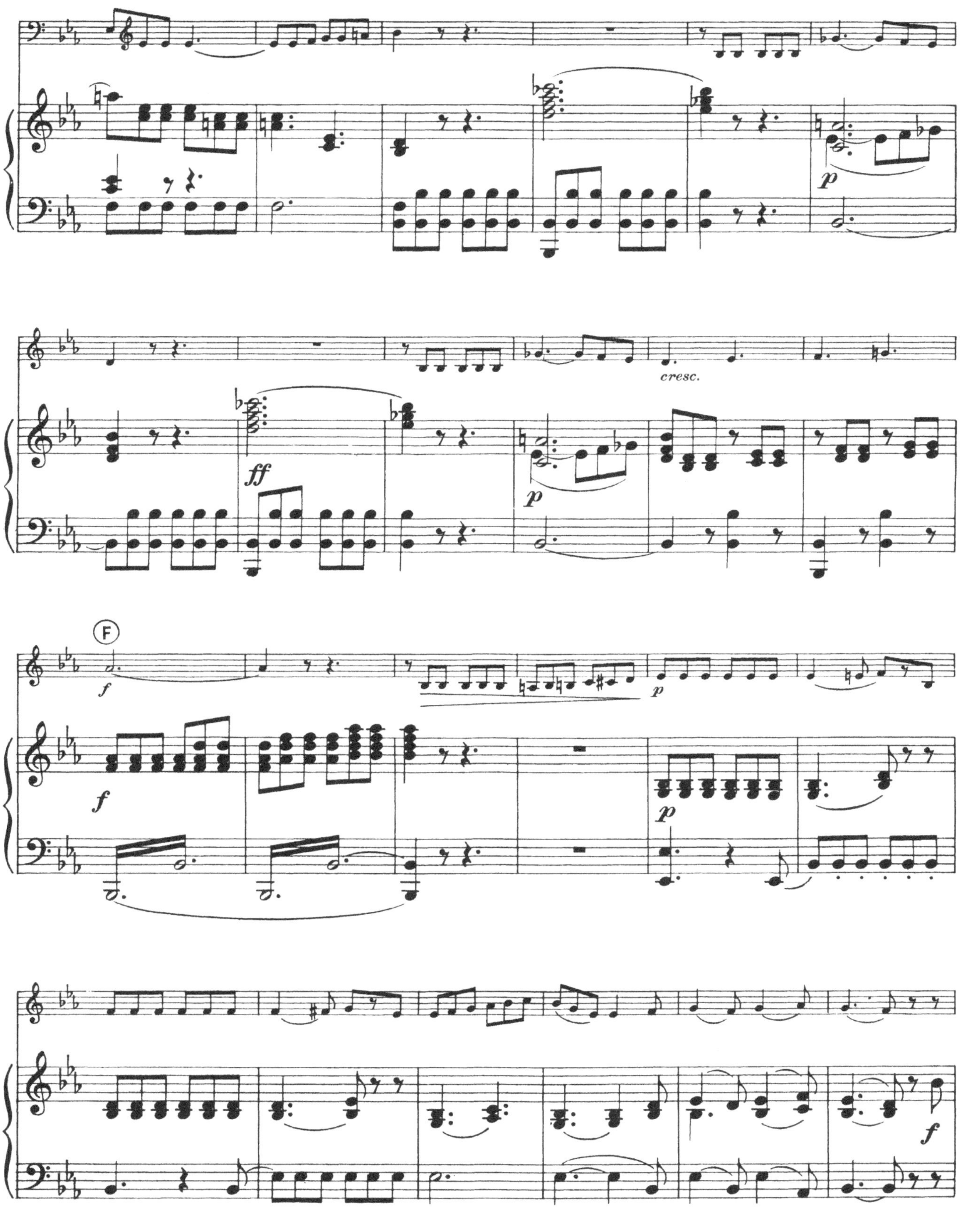
cresc.
F

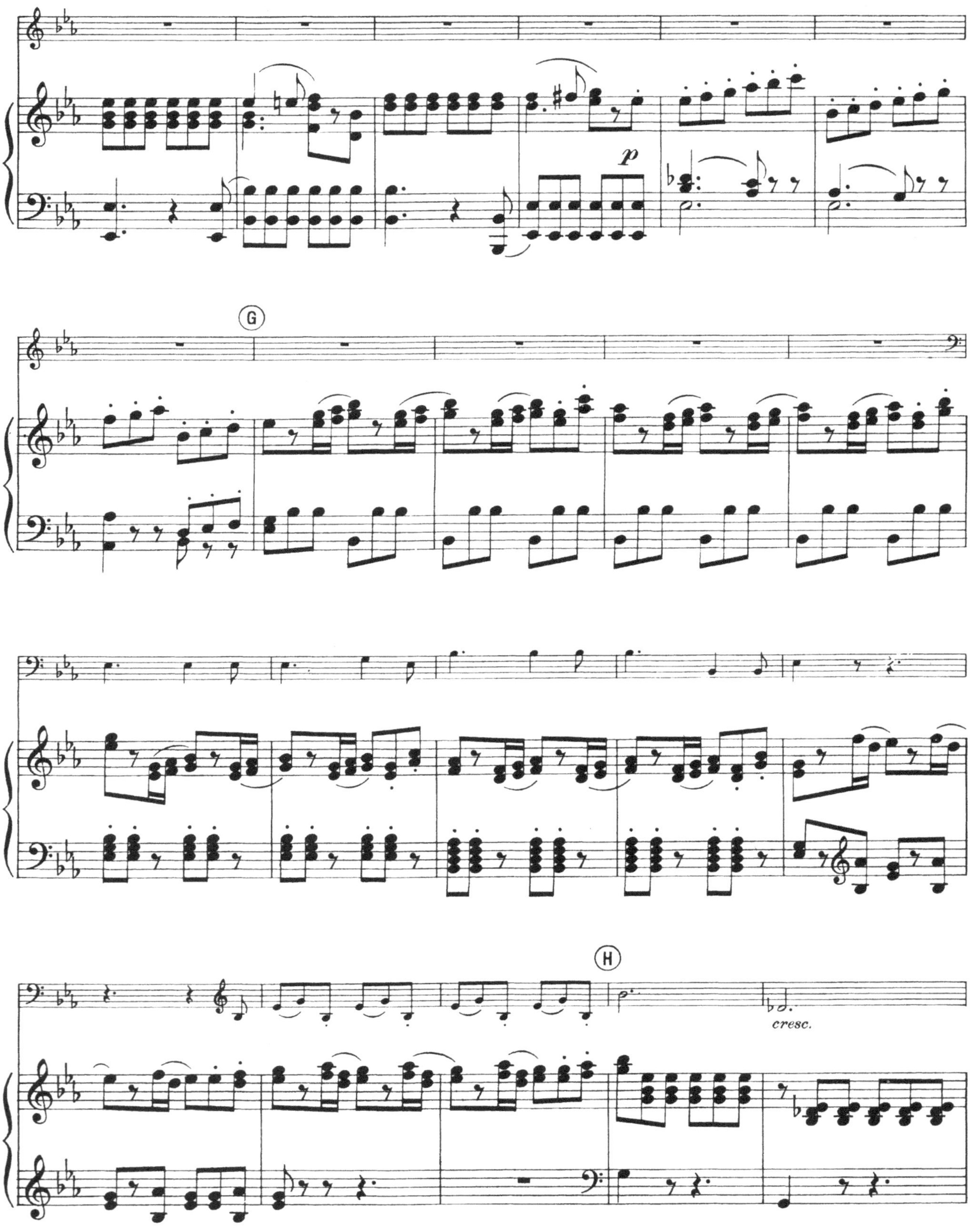
G
H
p
cresc.

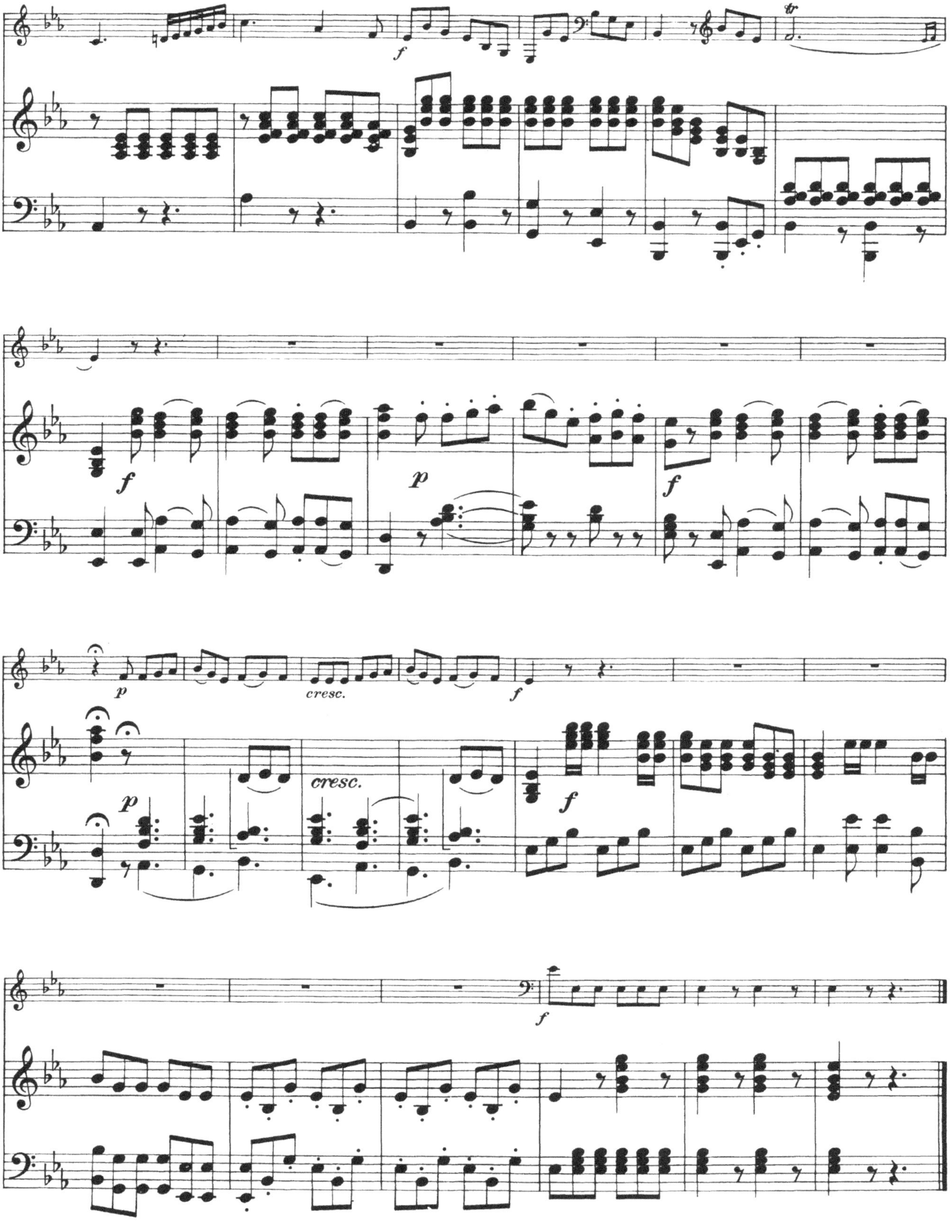
f
tr
f
p
f
p
p
cresc.
f
cresc.
f
f

Concerto No. 4 in E♭ Major
for Horn and Orchestra
[K. 495]

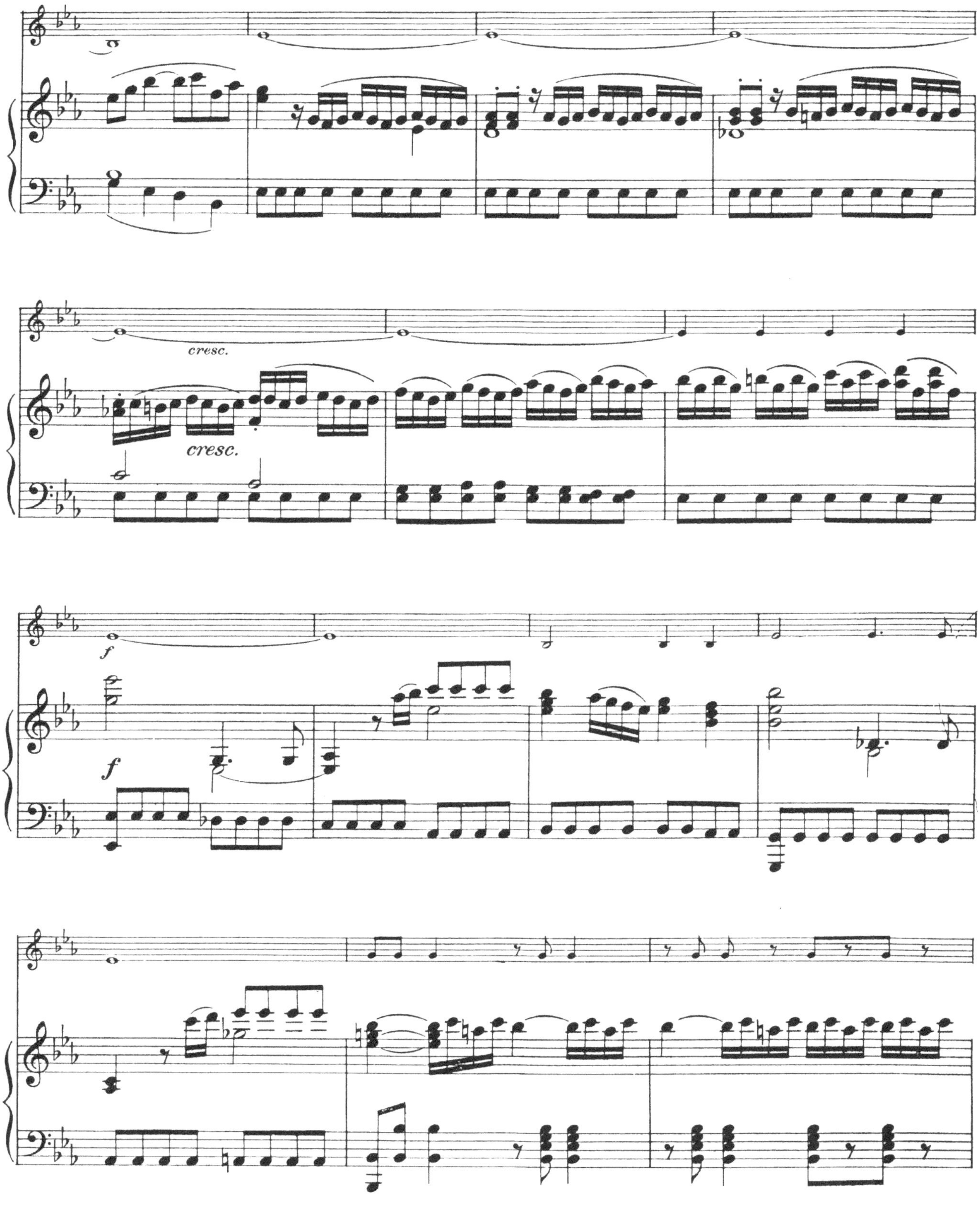
cresc.
cresc.
f
f

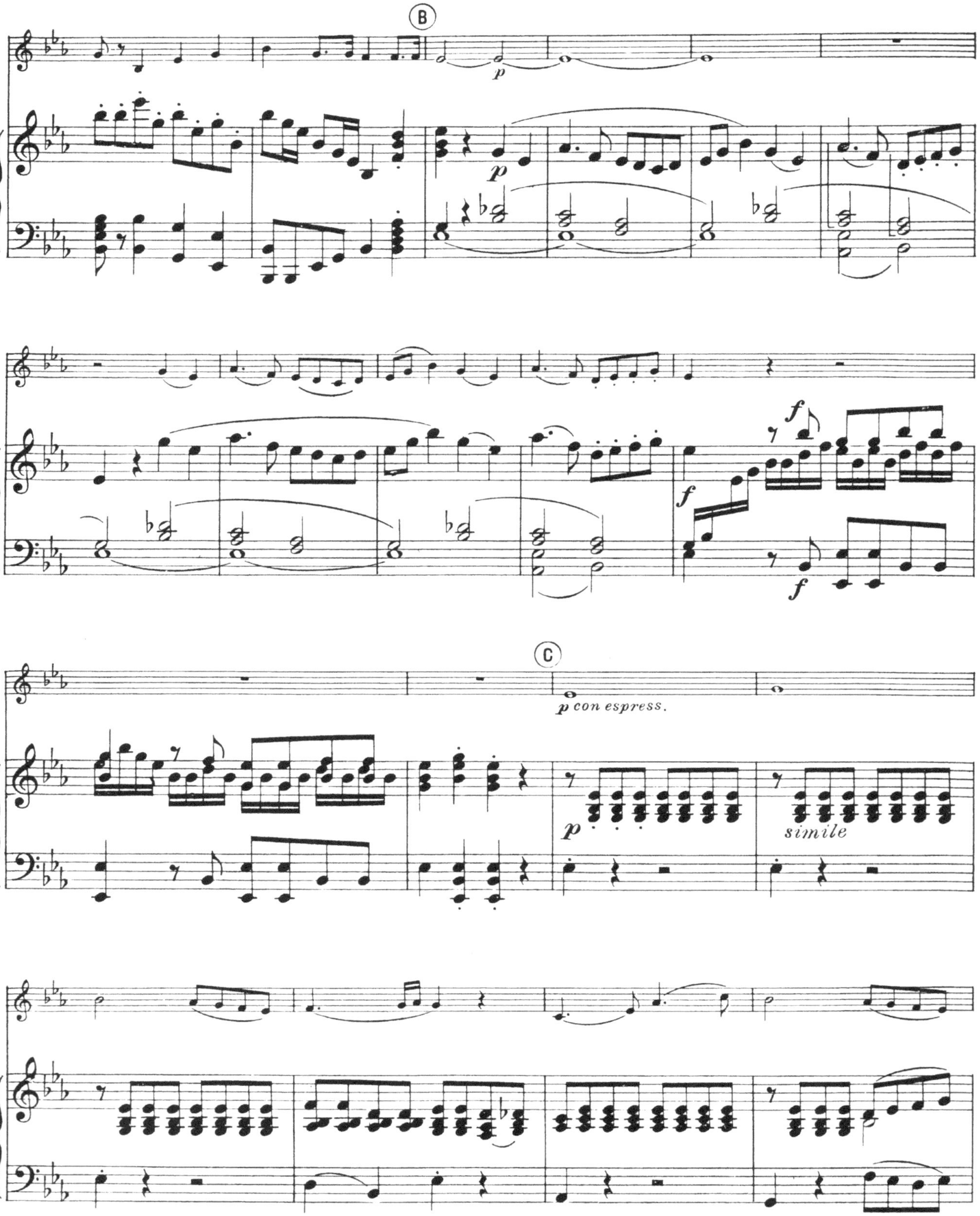
B
p
f
f
C
p con espress.
p
simile

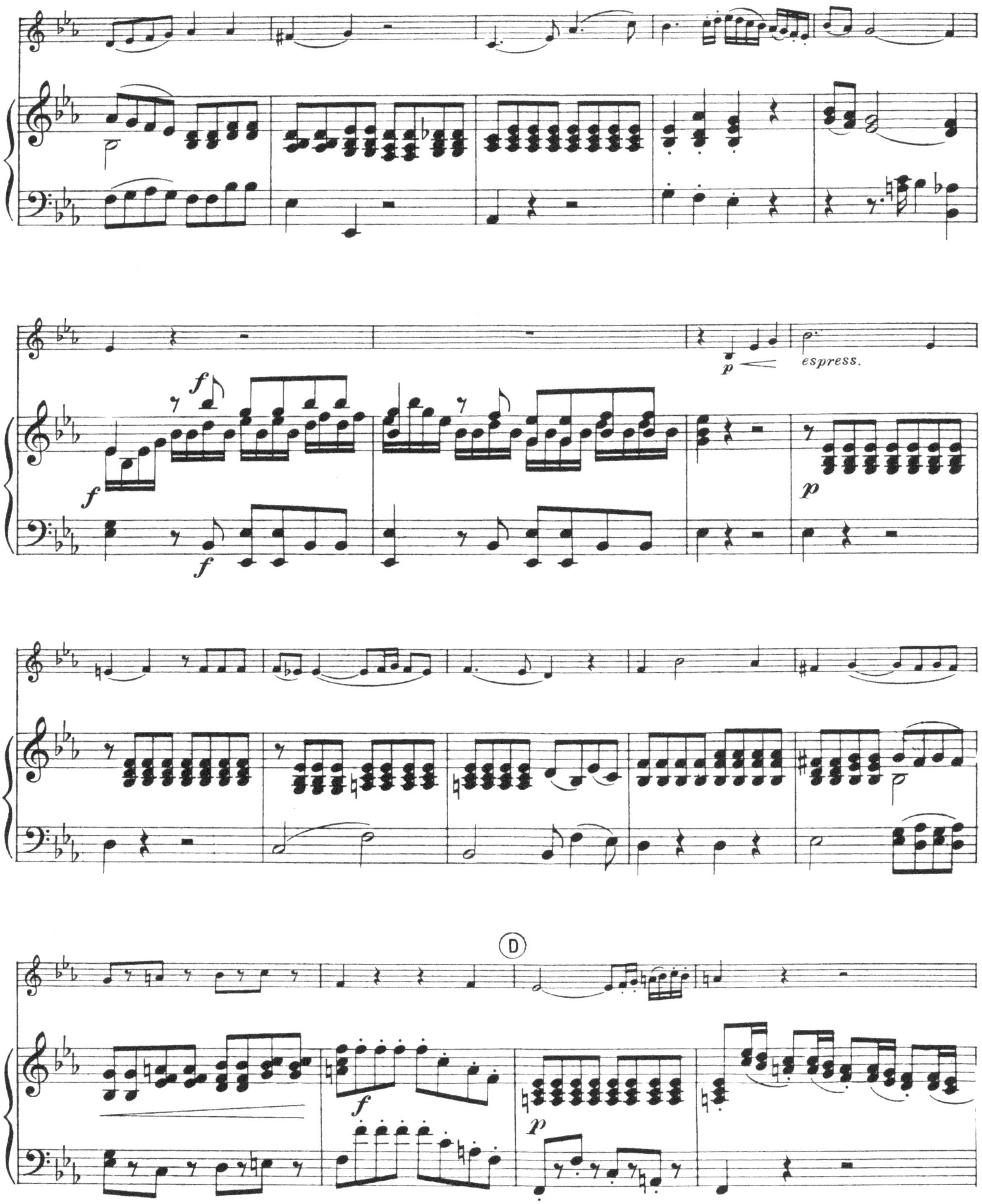
f
f
f
p
espress.
p
D
f
p

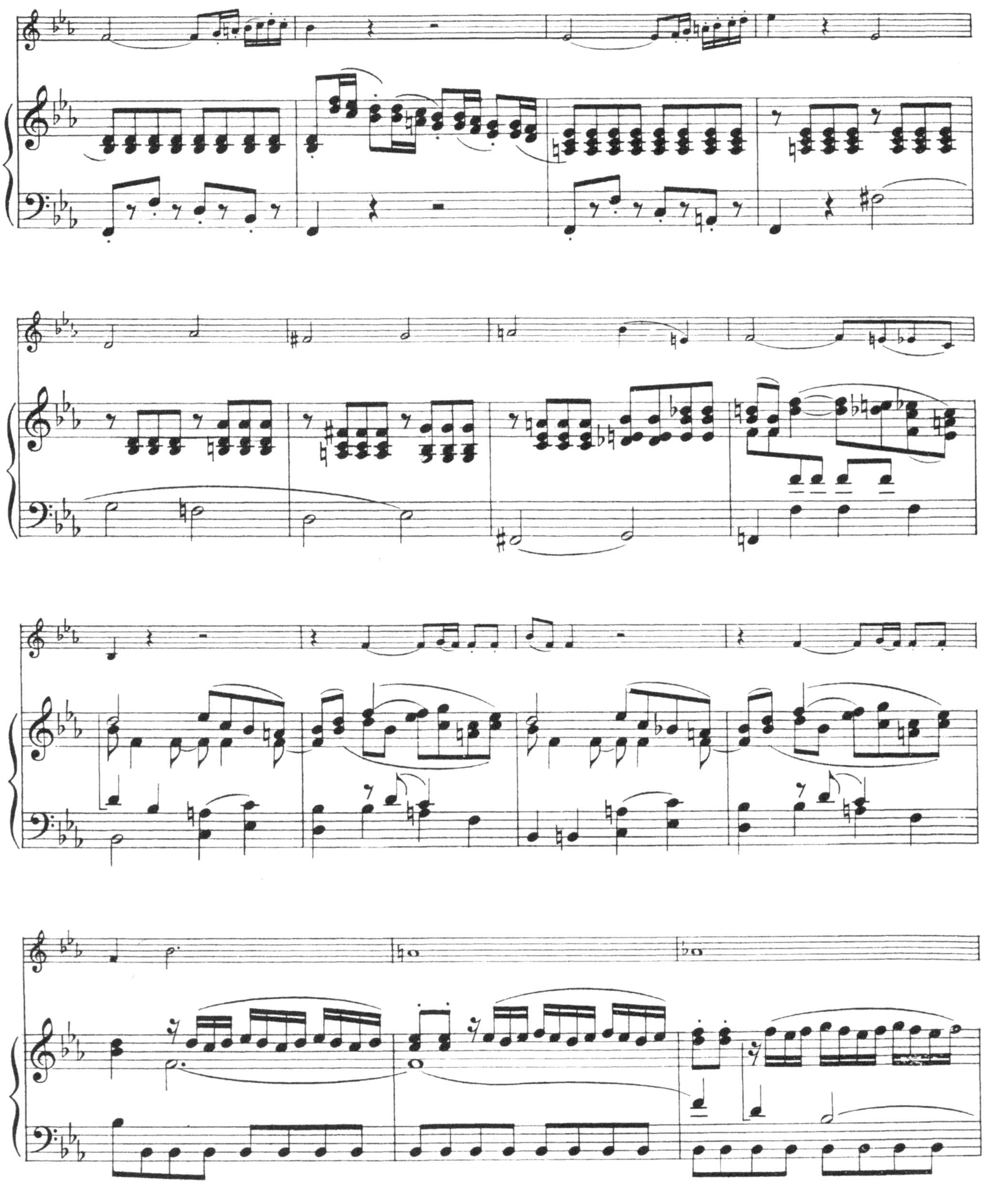

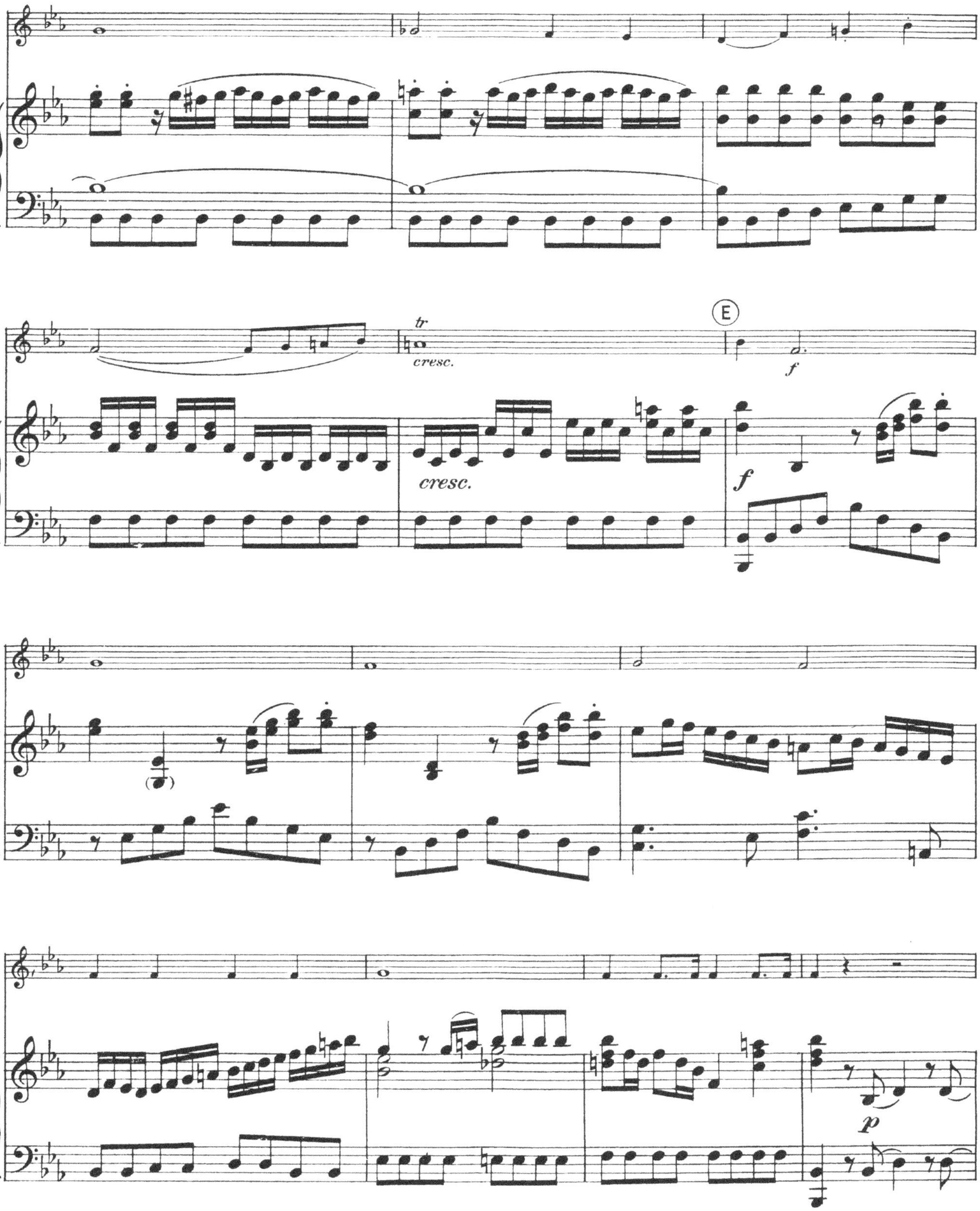
tr
cresc.
E
f
cresc.
f
p

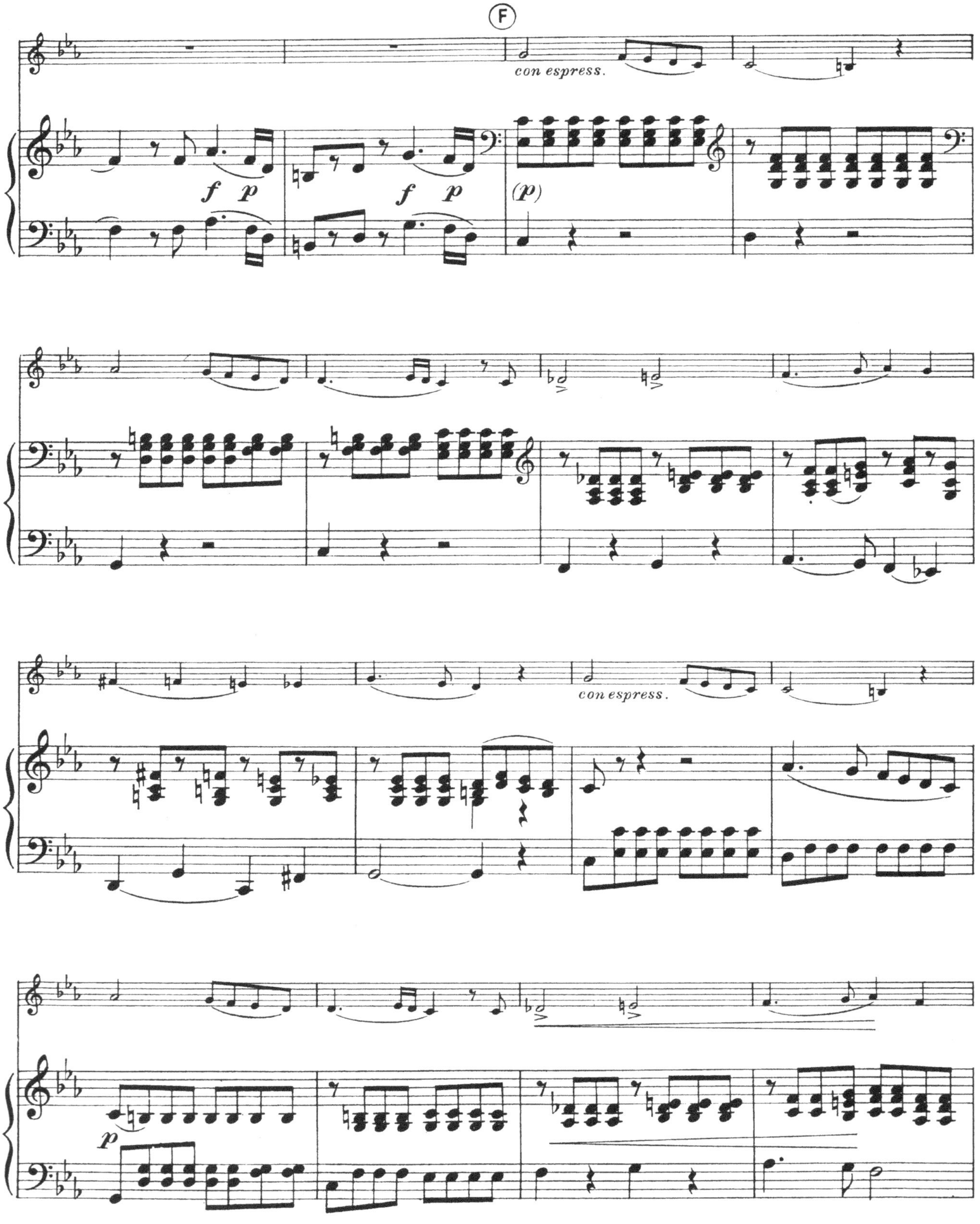
F
con espress.
f
p
f
p
(p)
con espress.
p

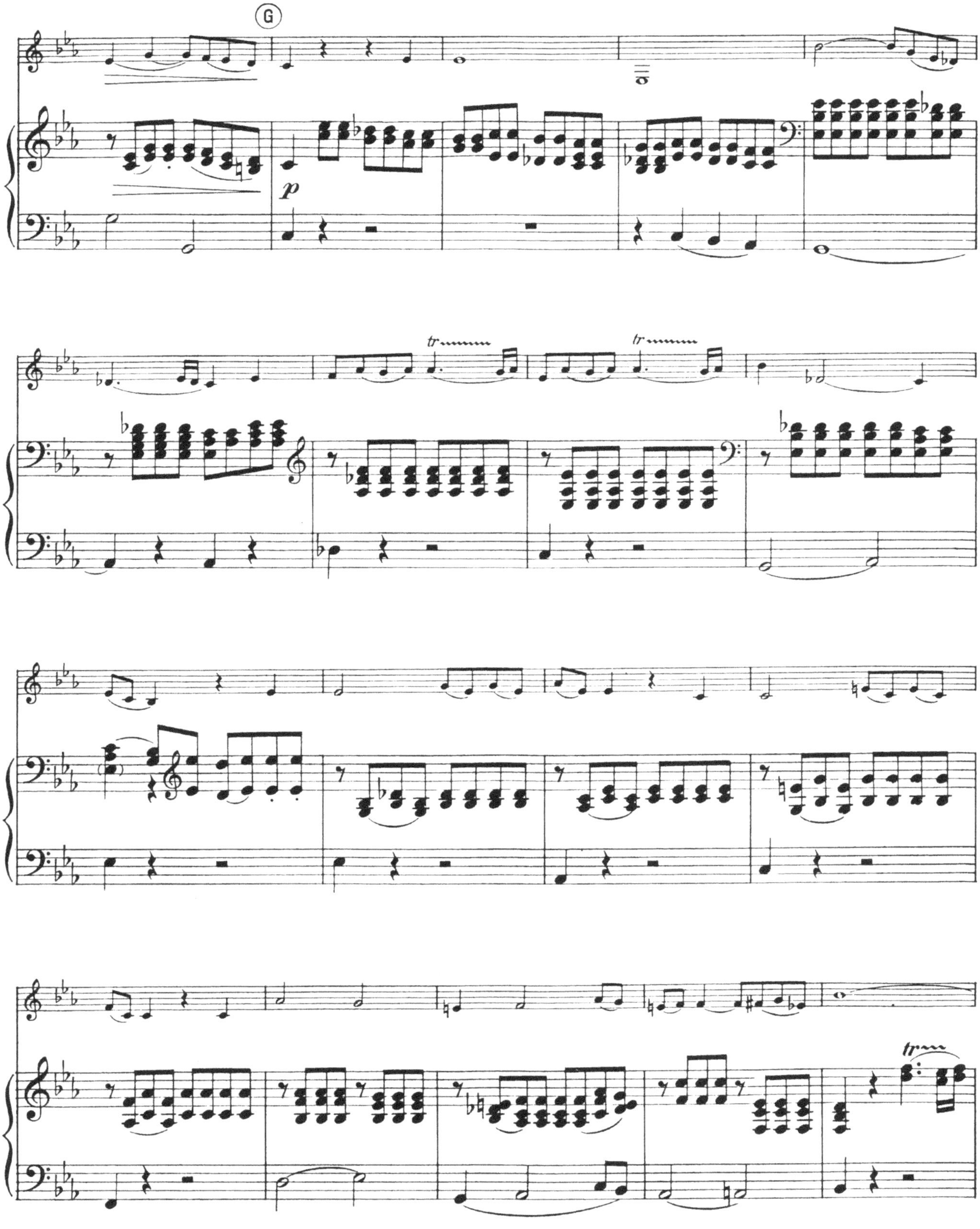
G
p
tr
tr
tr

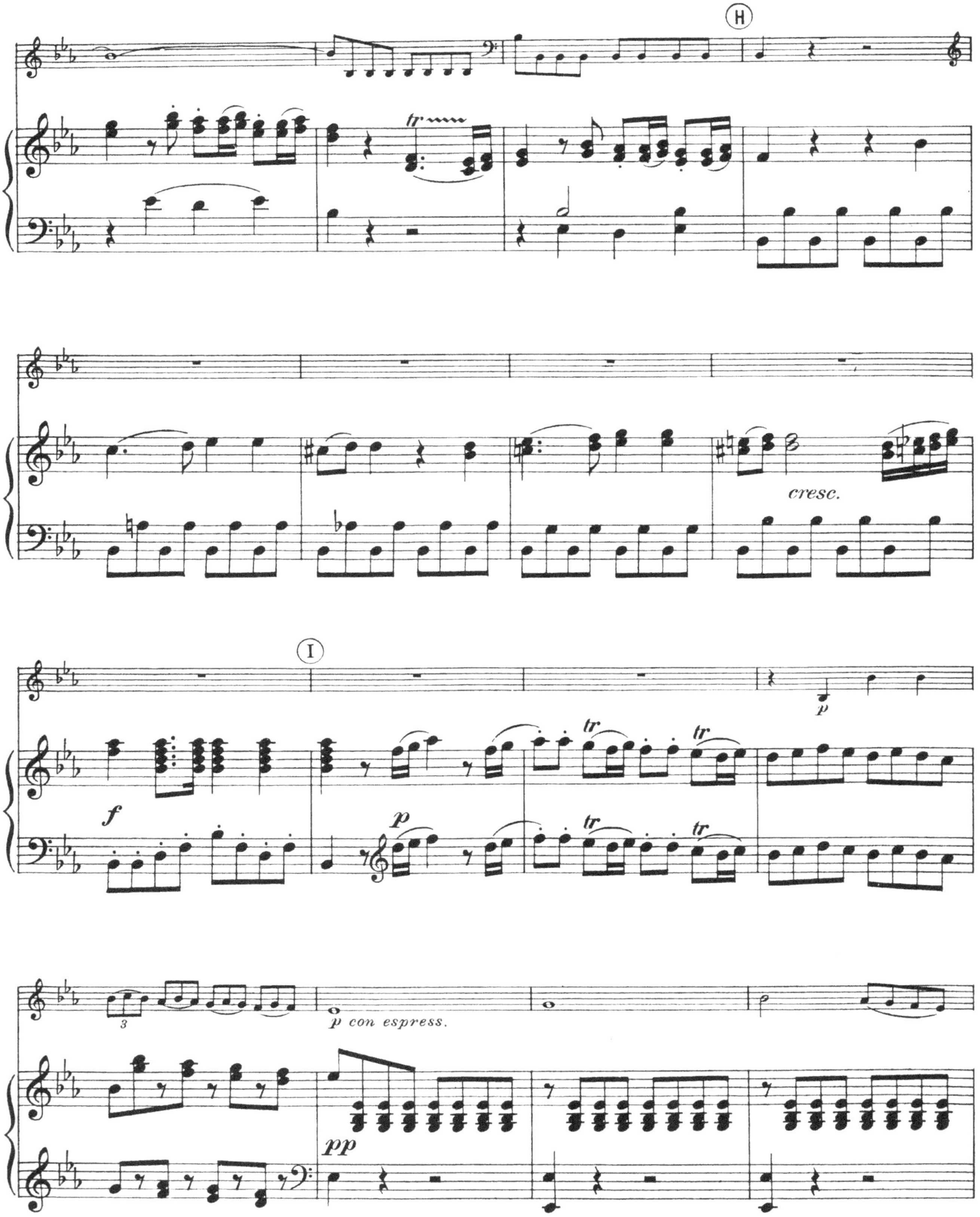
H
tr
cresc.
I
f
p
tr
tr
p
3
p con espress.
pp

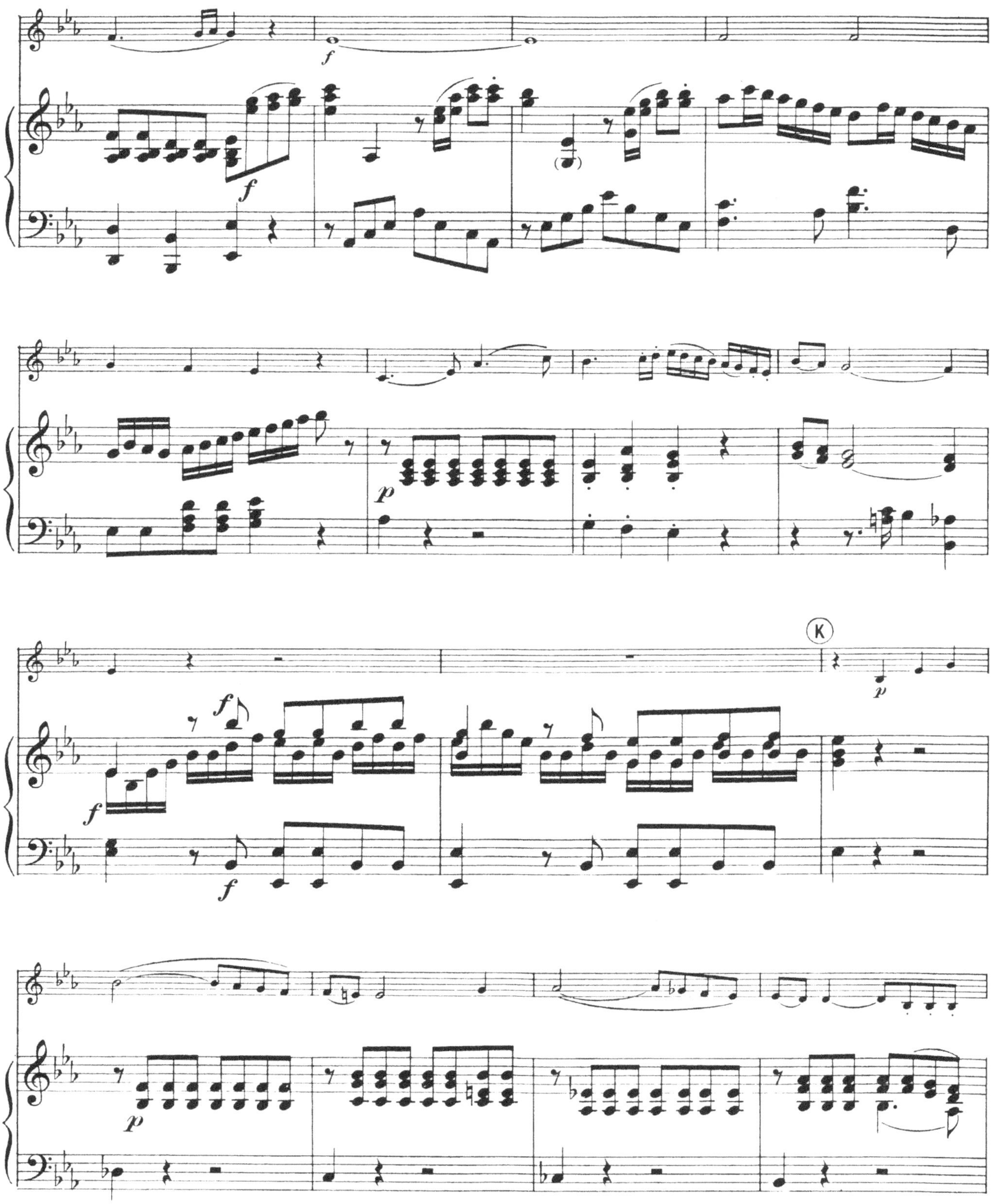
f
f
f
p
K
f
f
p
p

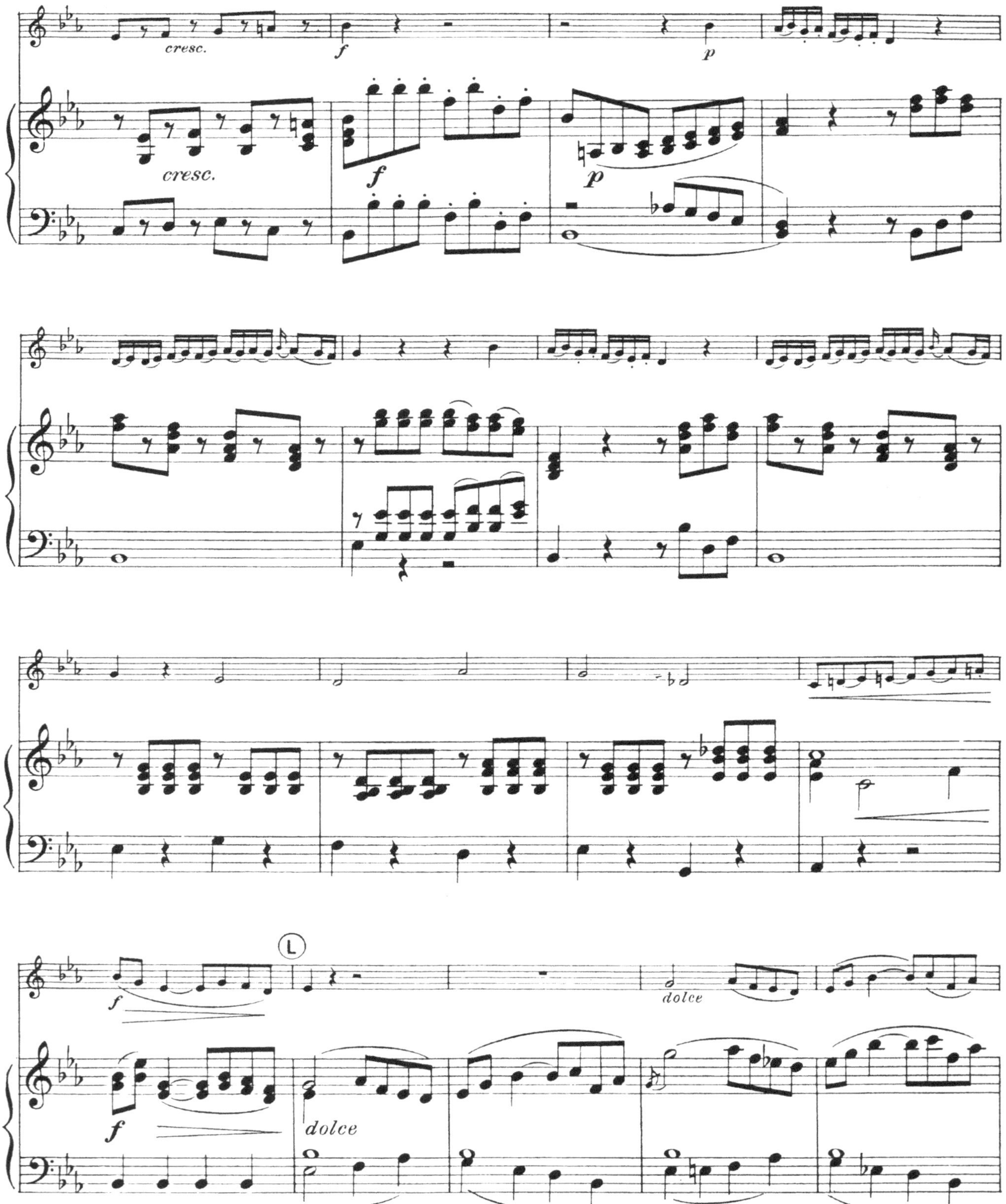
cresc.
f
p
L
dolce

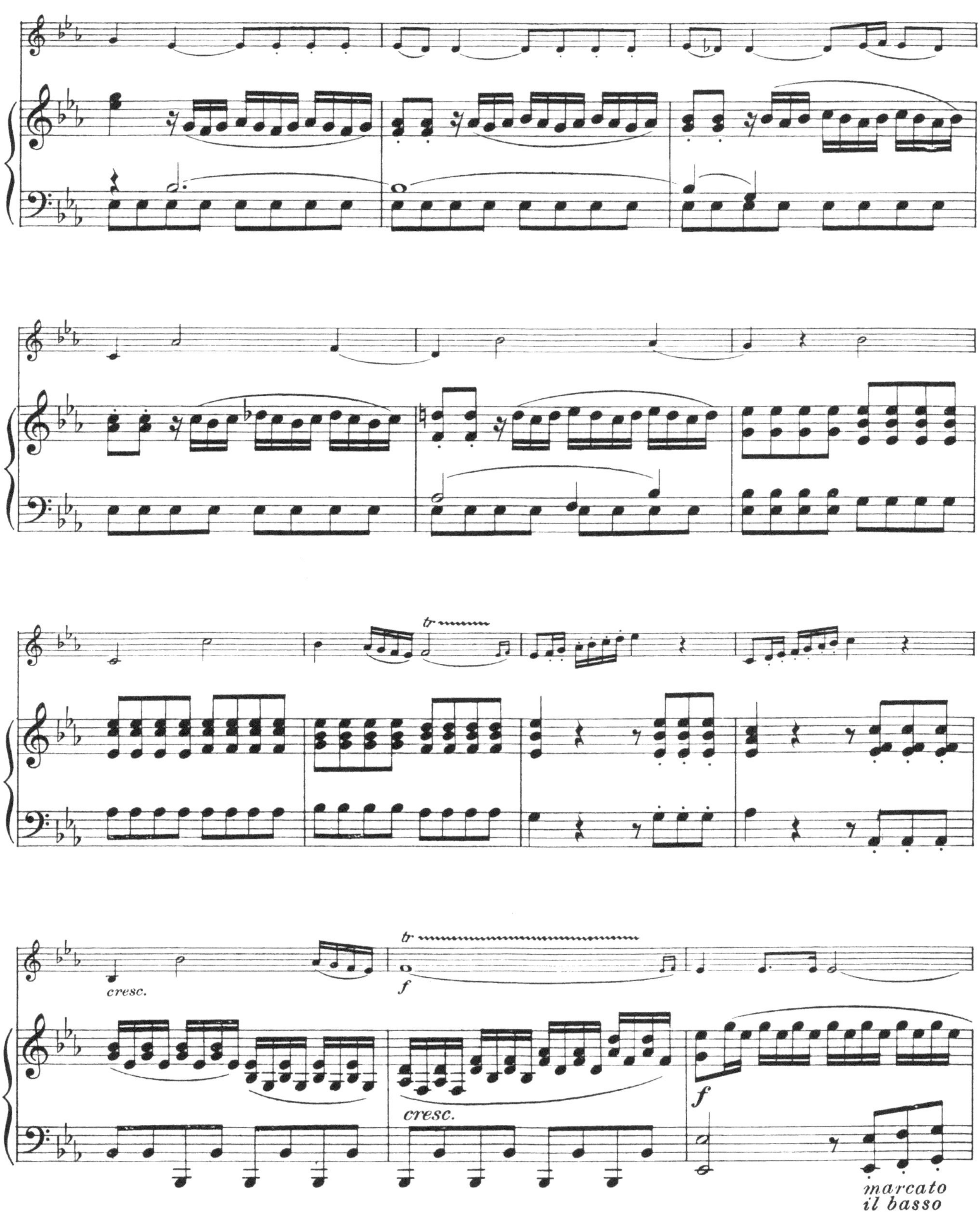
tr
tr
cresc.
f
cresc.
f
marcato
il basso

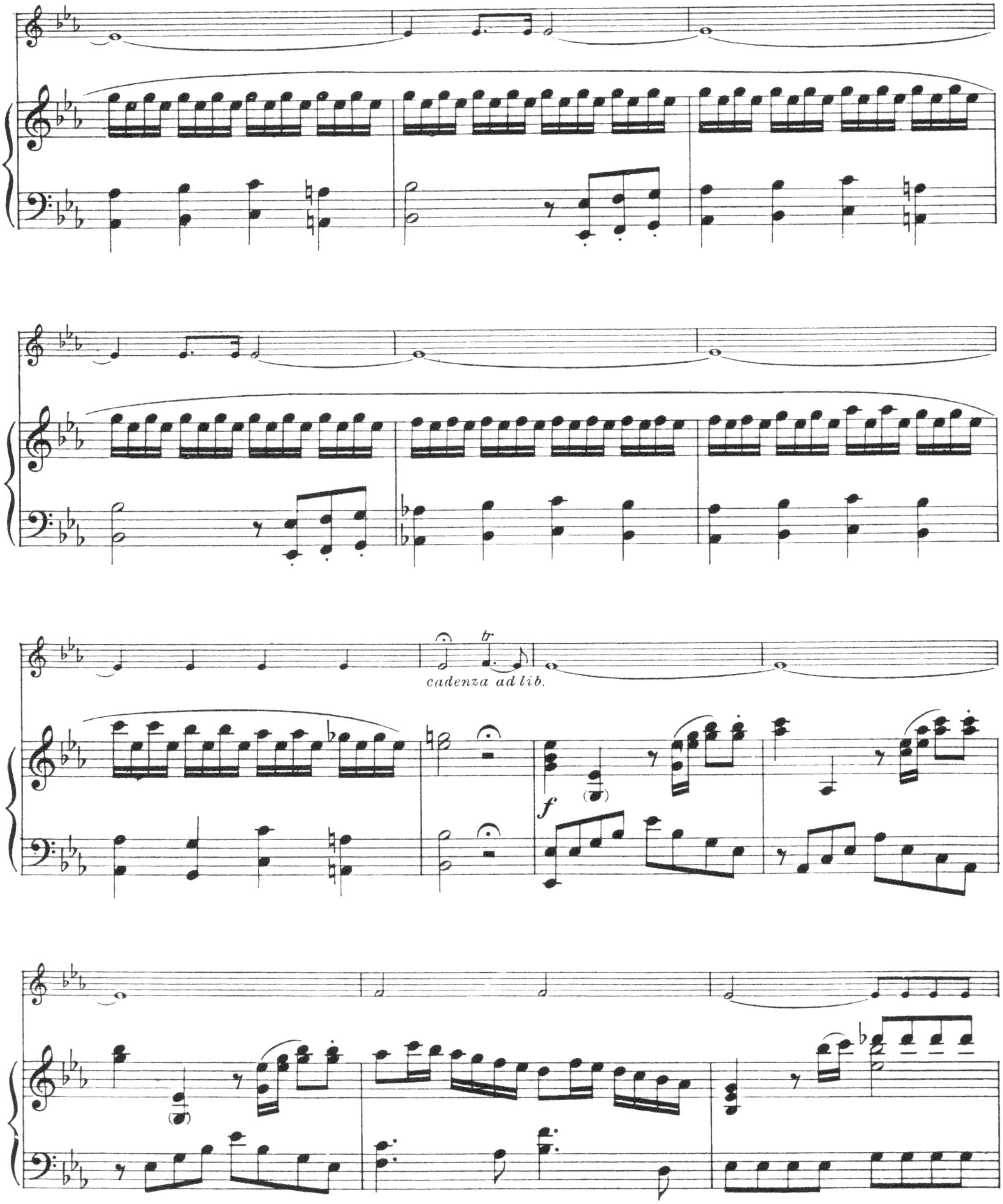
tr
cadenza ad lib.
f

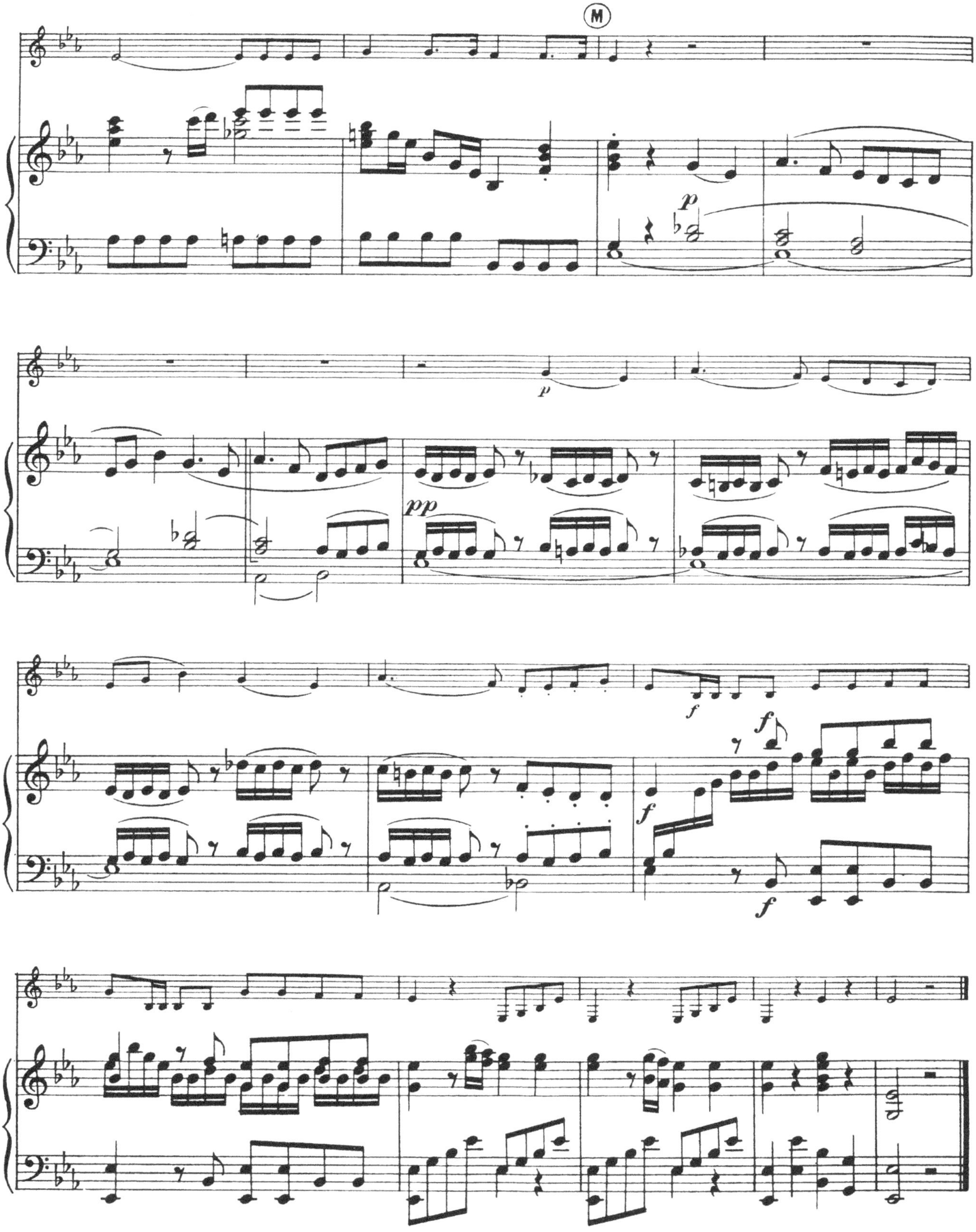
M
p
pp
f

Romanza

Andante

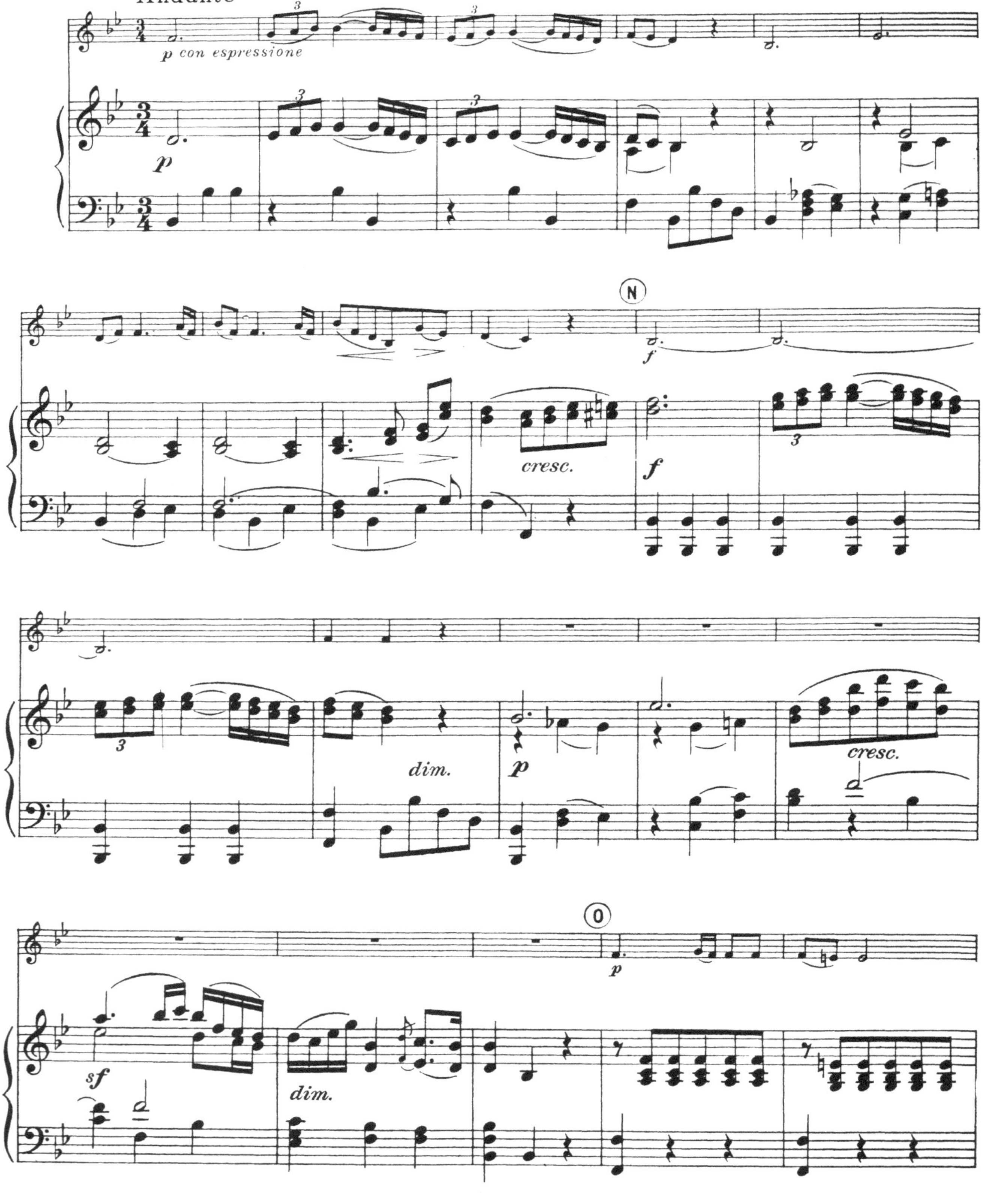

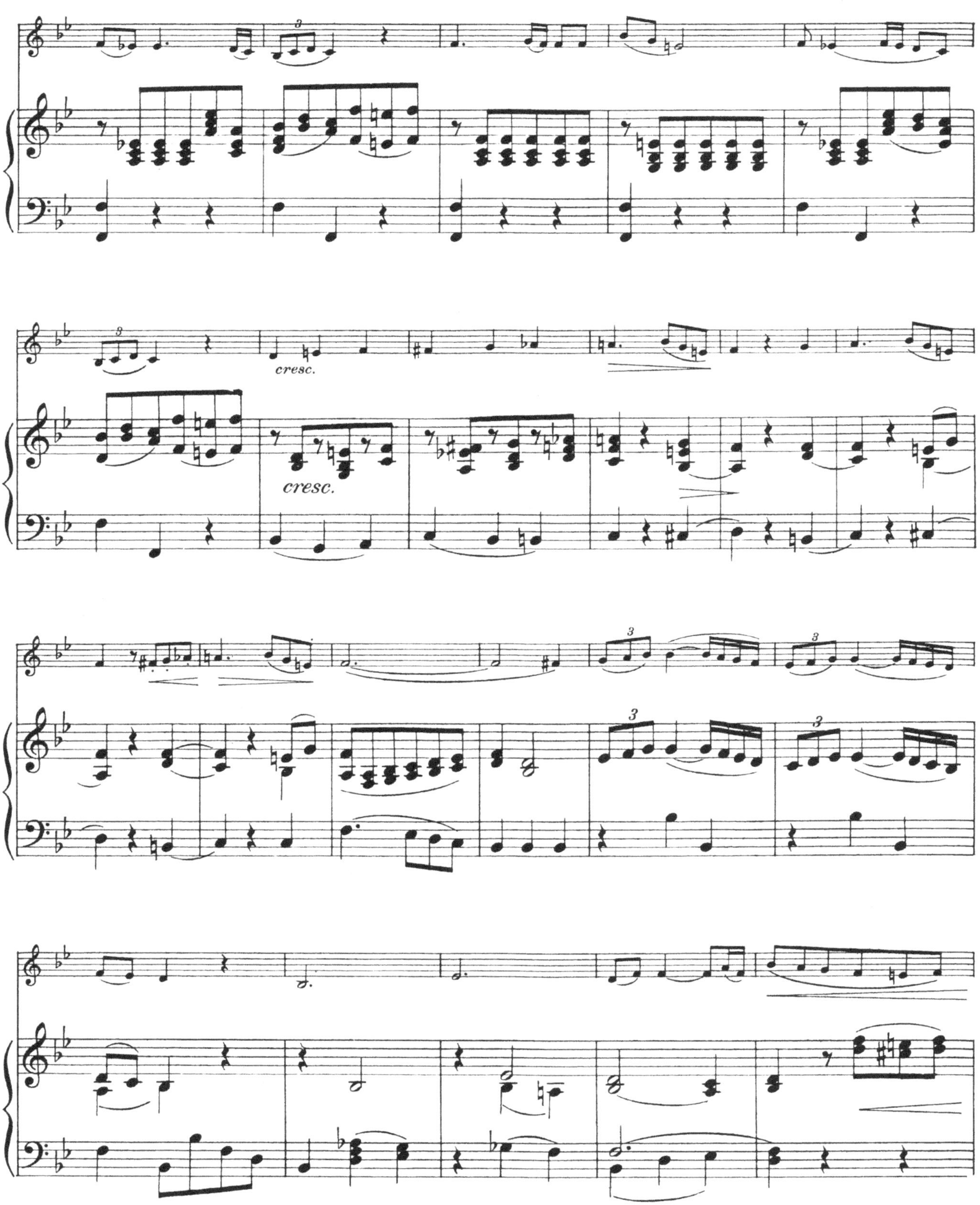
3
cresc.
cresc.

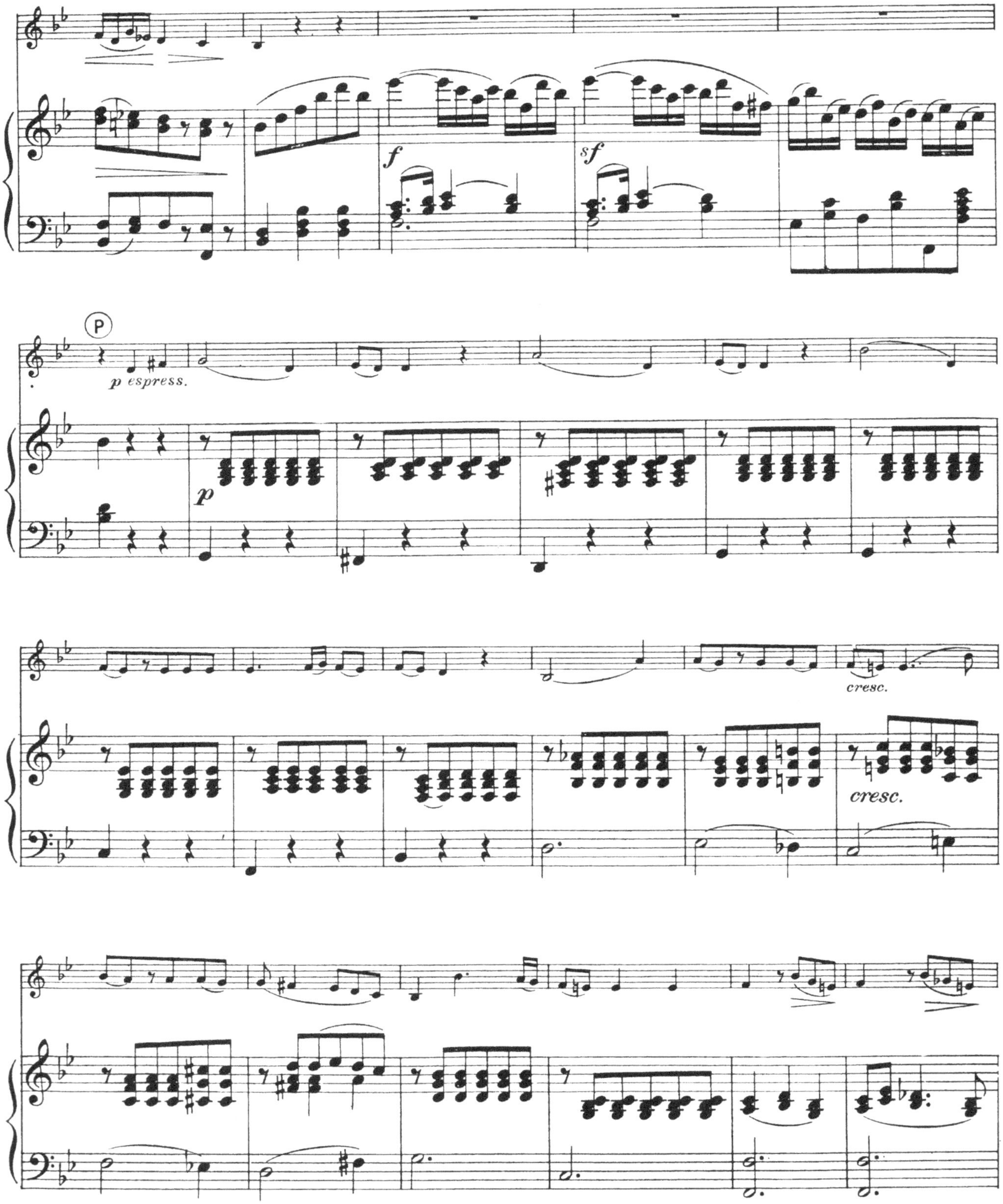
f
sf
P
p espress.
p
cresc.
cresc.

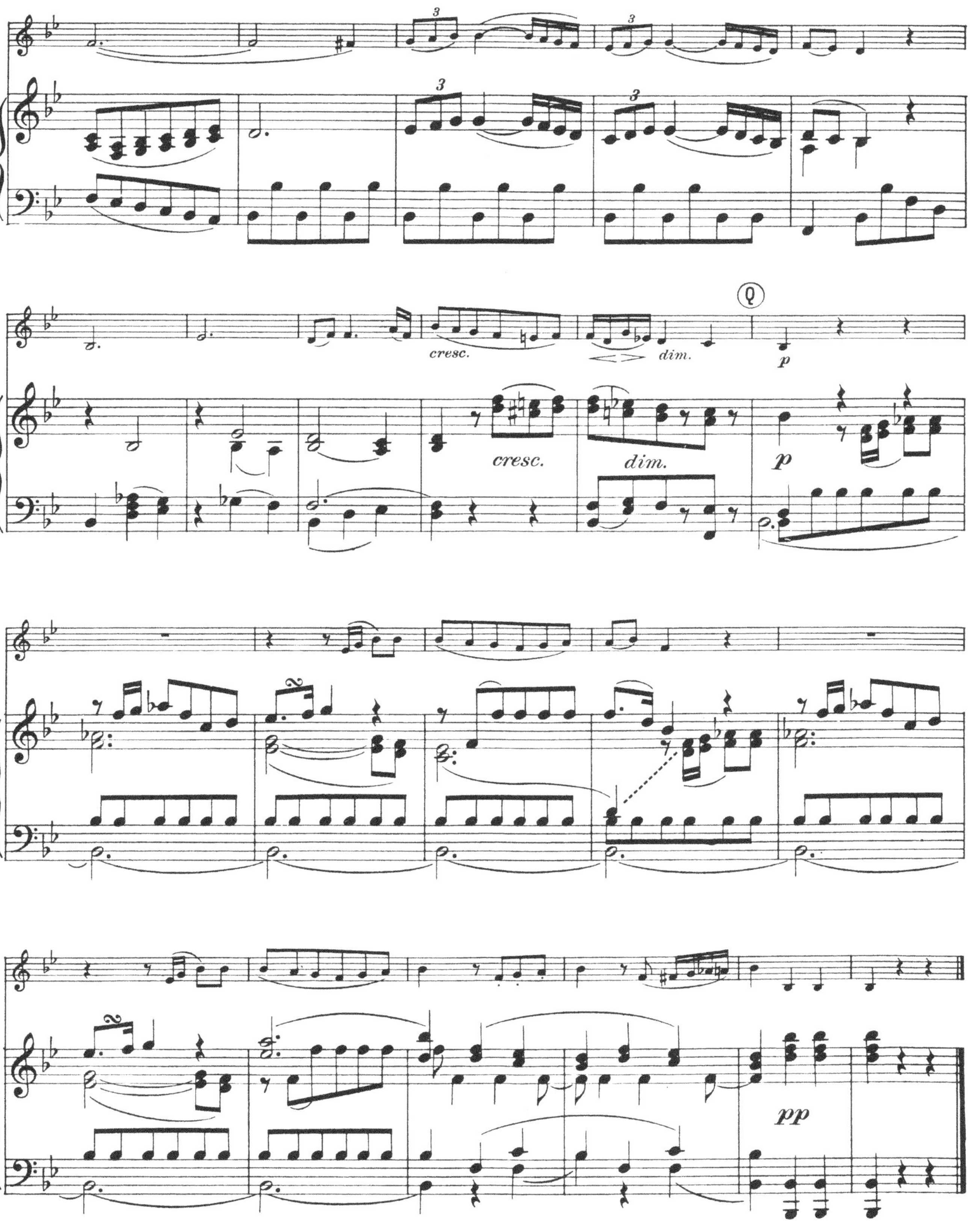
3
3
3
3
Q
cresc.
dim.
p
cresc.
dim.
p
pp

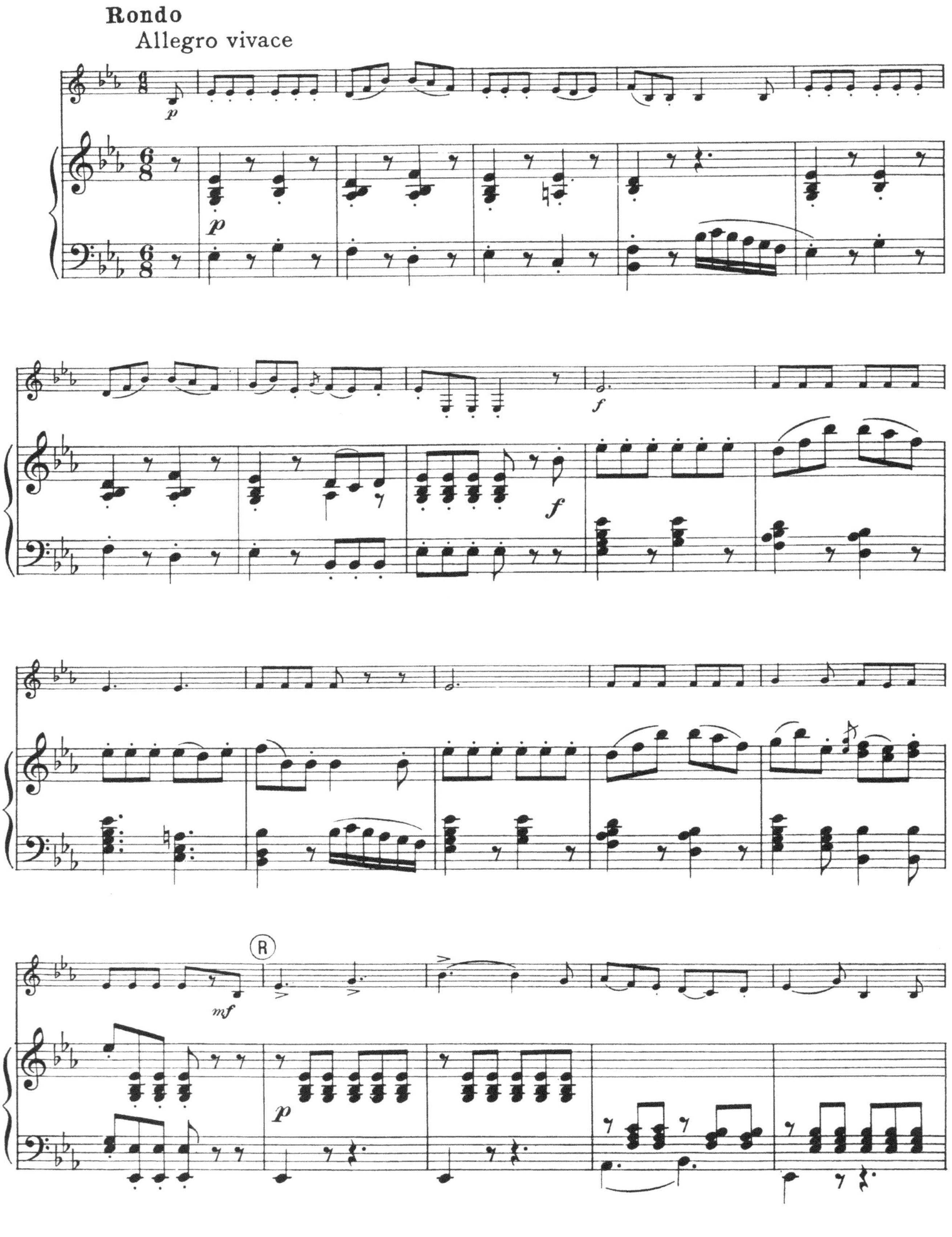
Rondo
Allegro vivace
p
p
f
f
mf
R
p

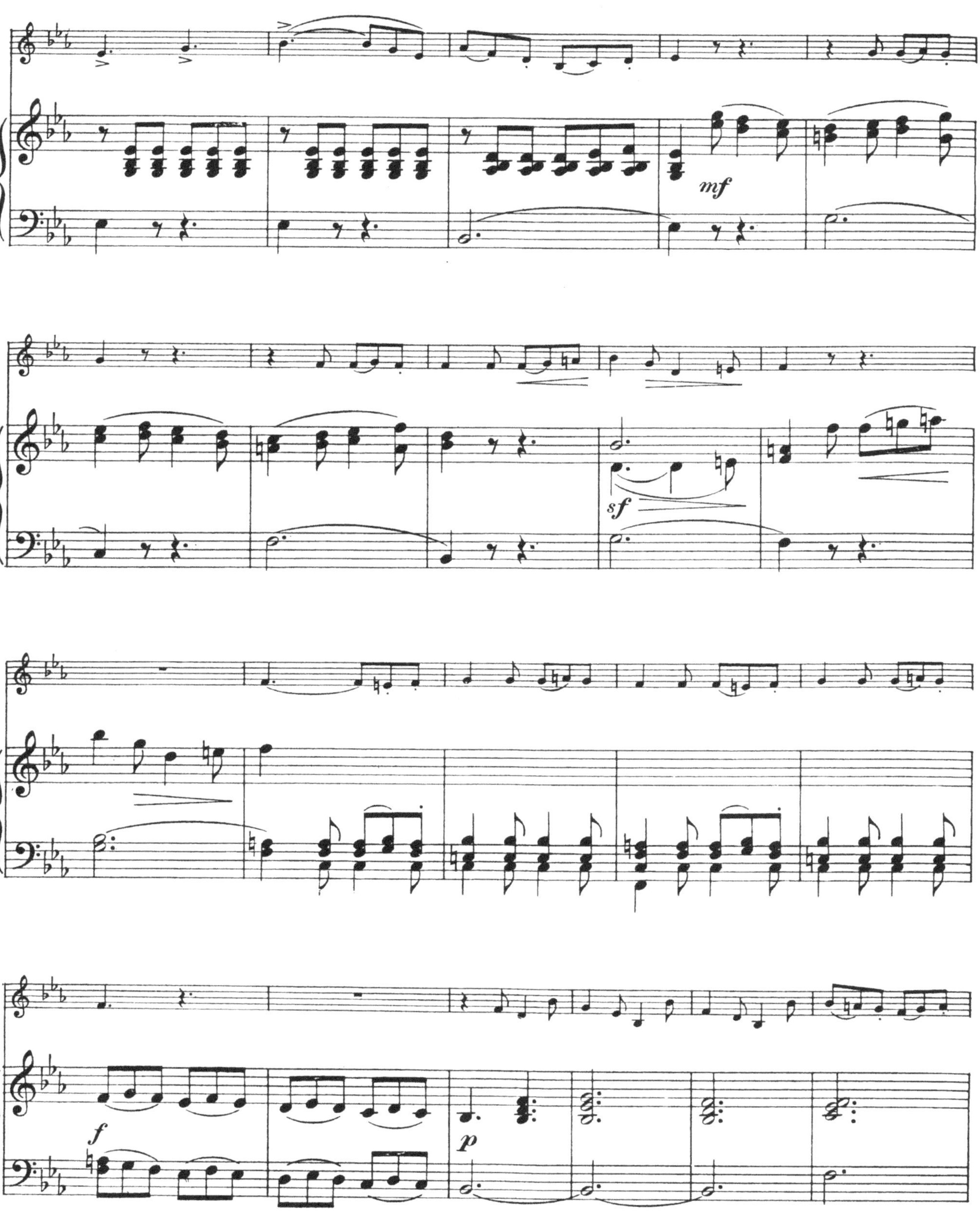
mf
sf
f
p

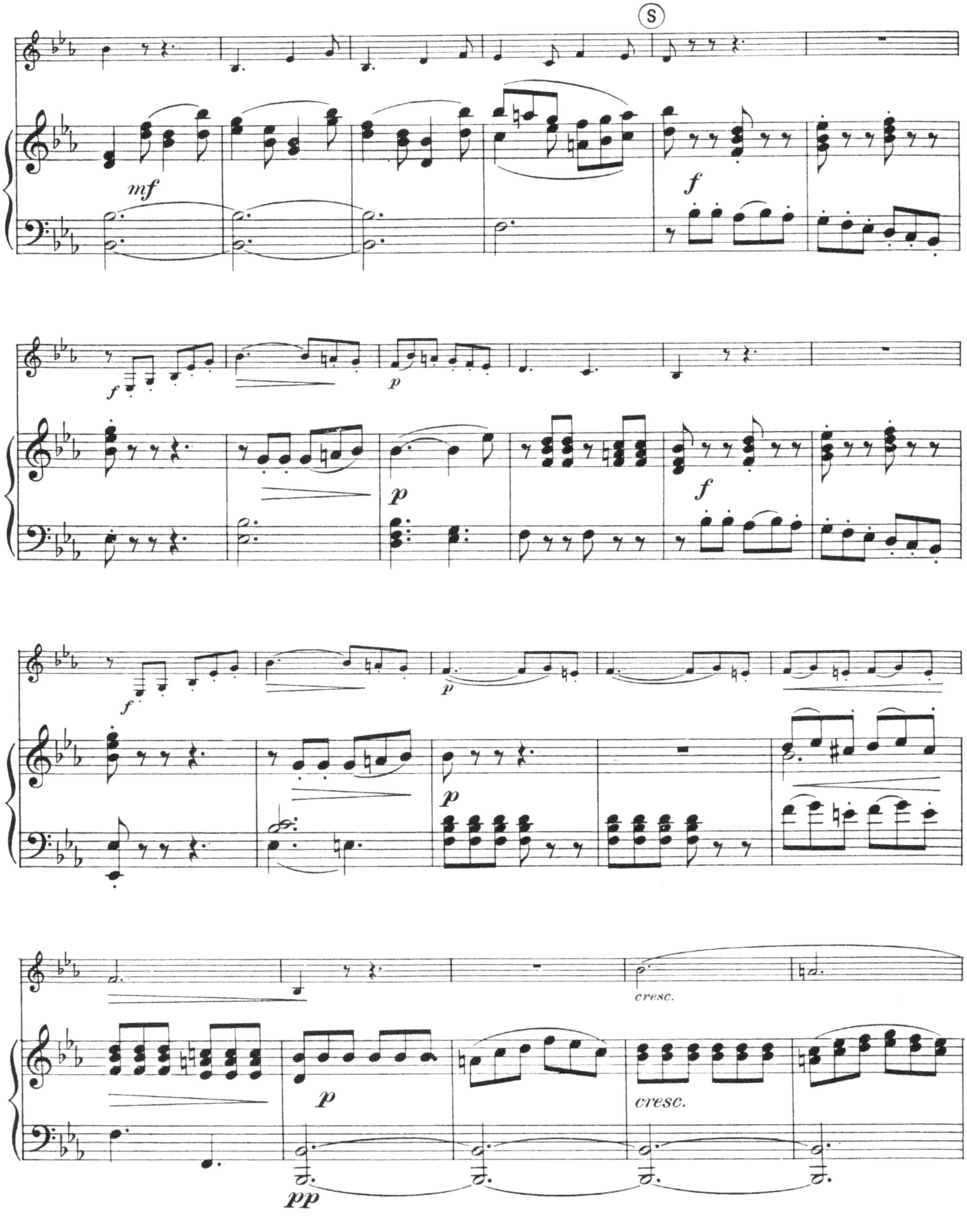
S
mf
f
p
cresc.
pp

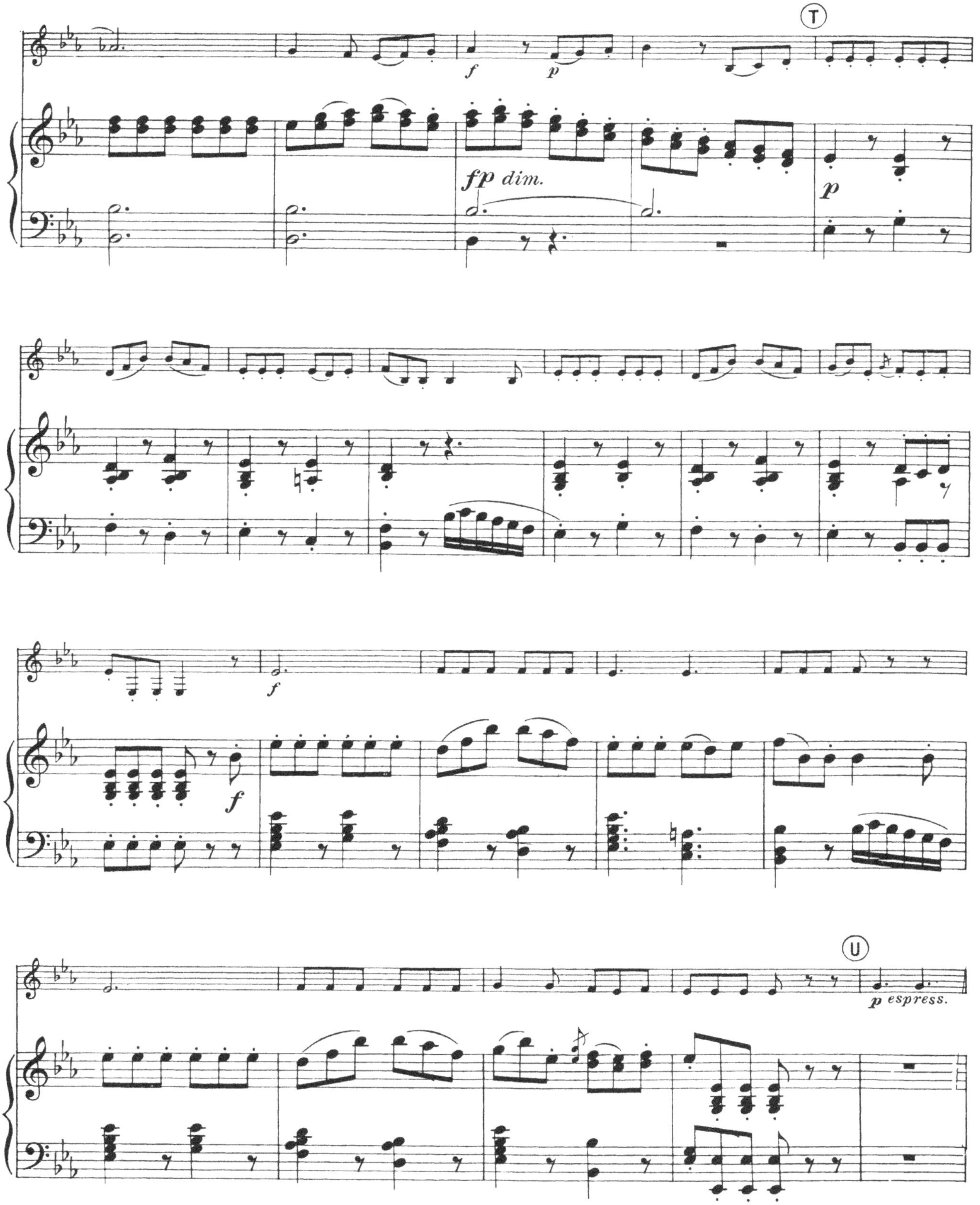
T
f
p
fp dim.
p
f
f
U
p espress.

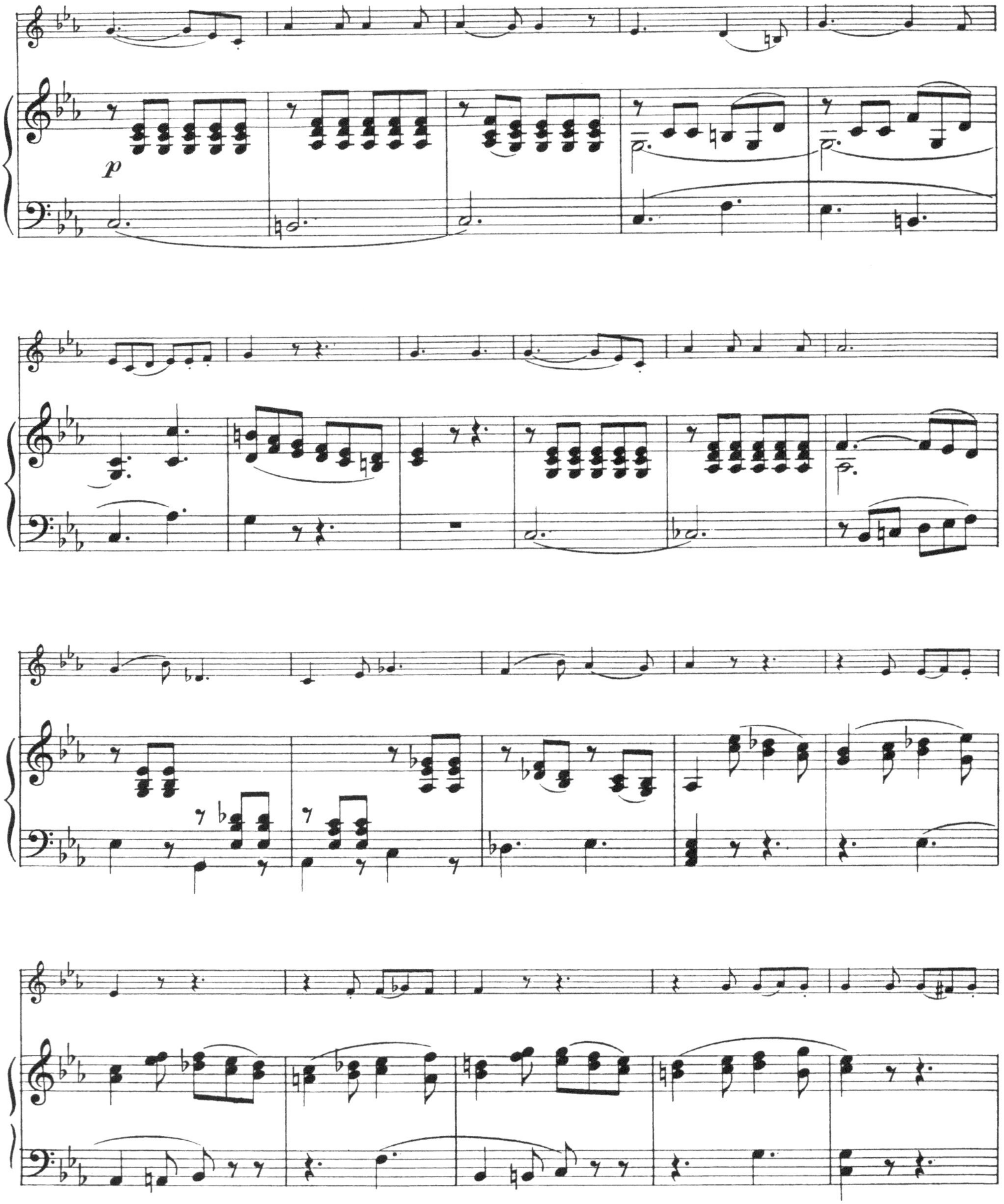
p

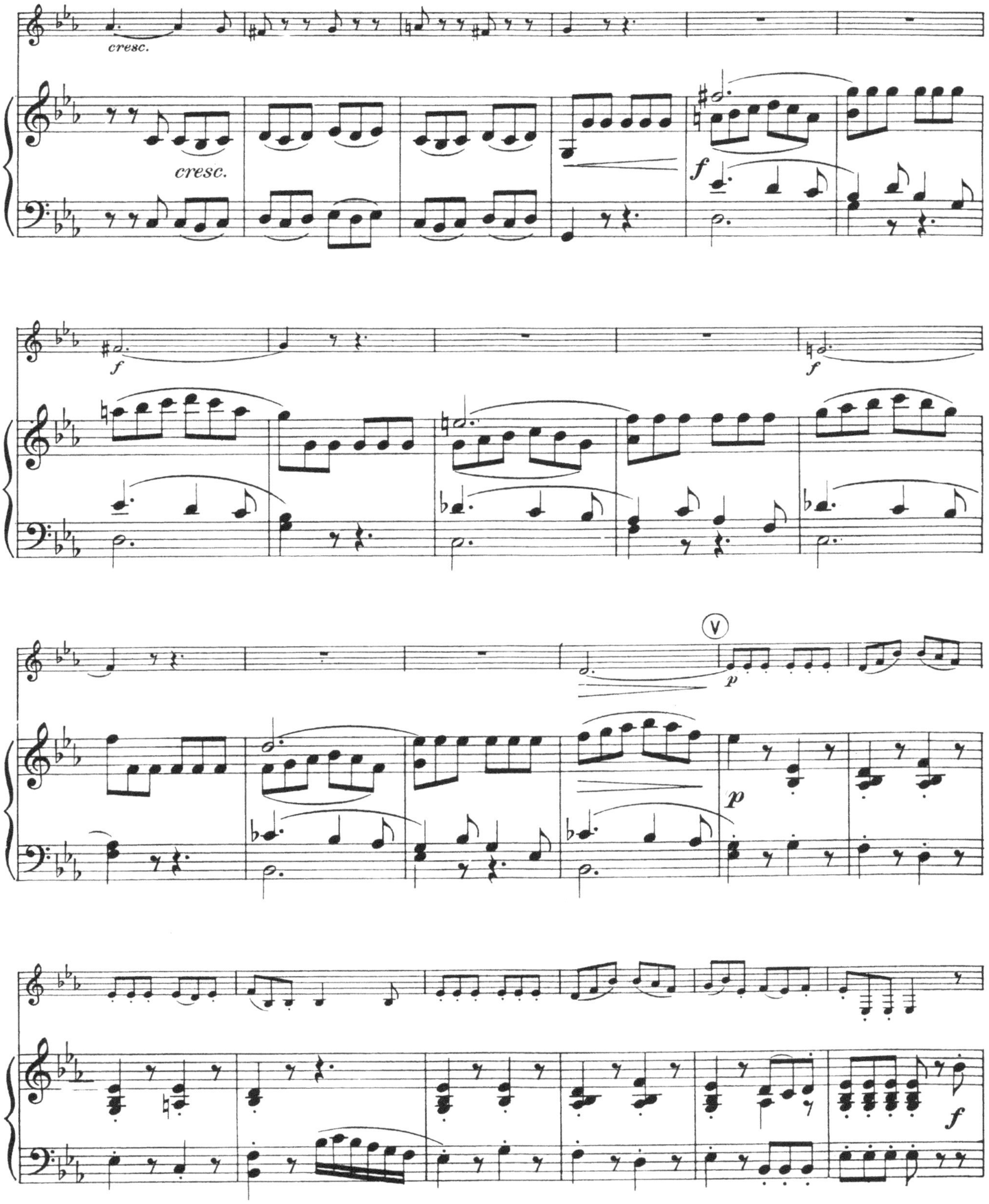
cresc.
cresc.
f
f
f
f
V
p
p
f

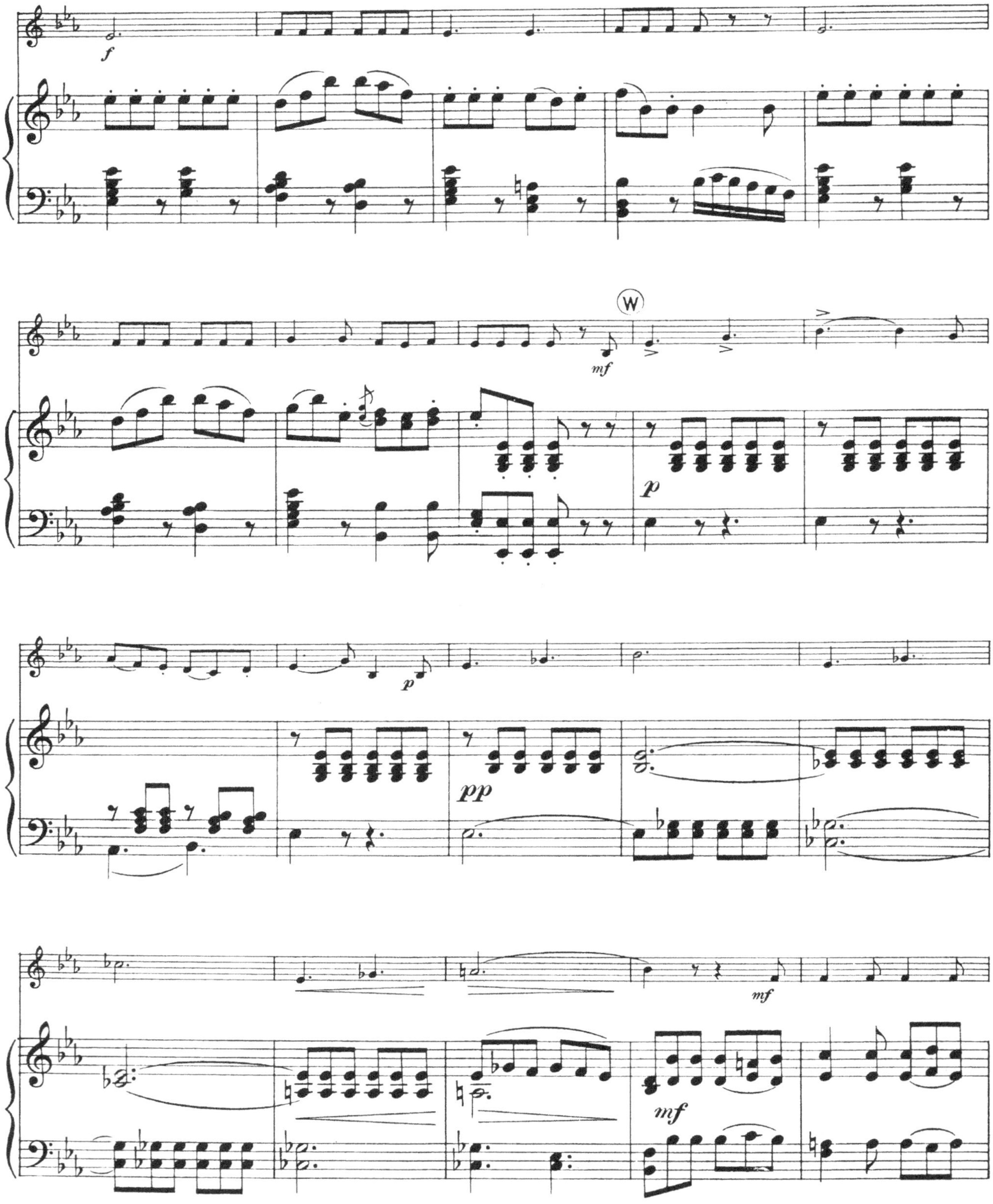
W
f
mf
p
pp
mf

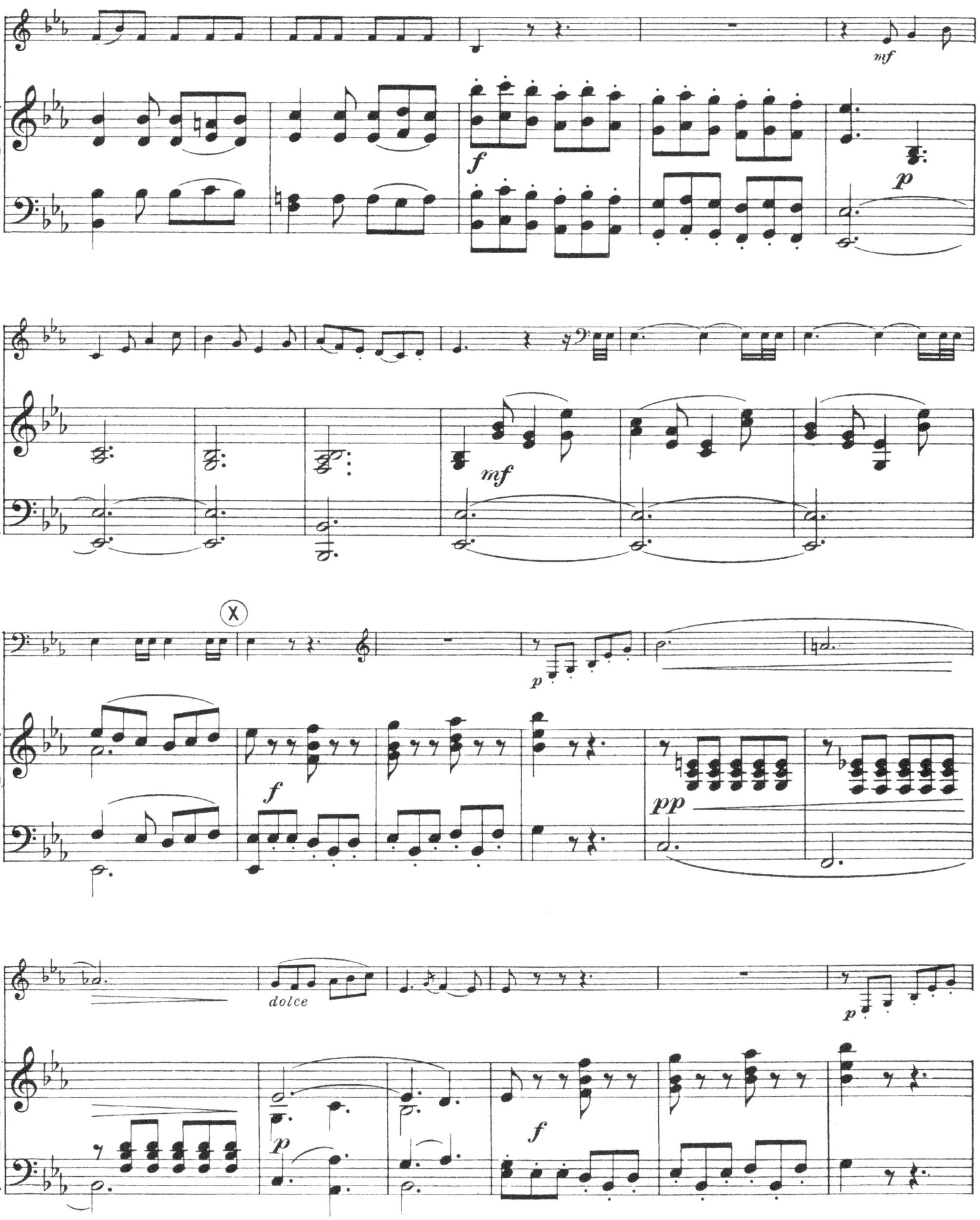
mf
f
p
mf
X
p
pp
dolce
p
f
p

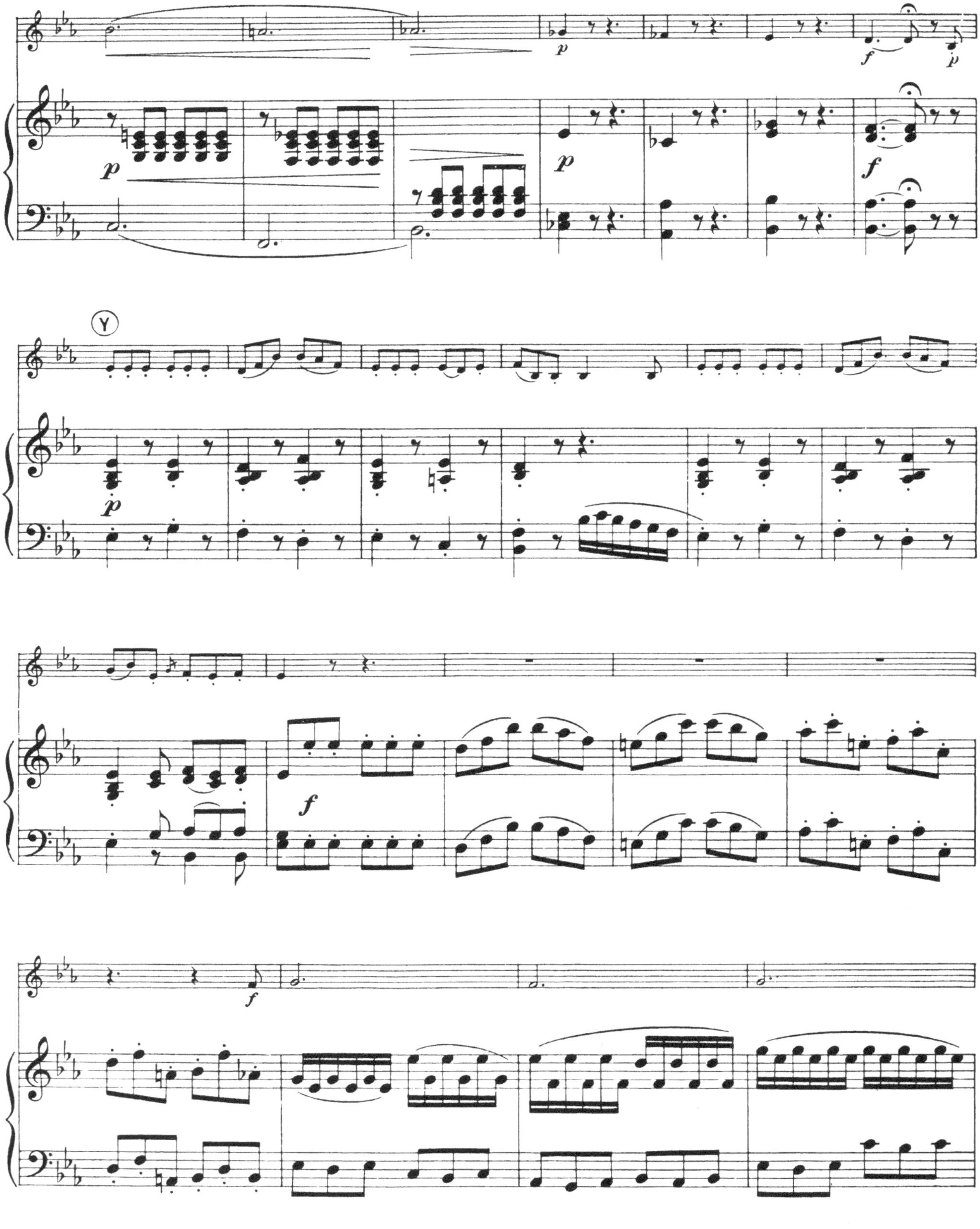
Y

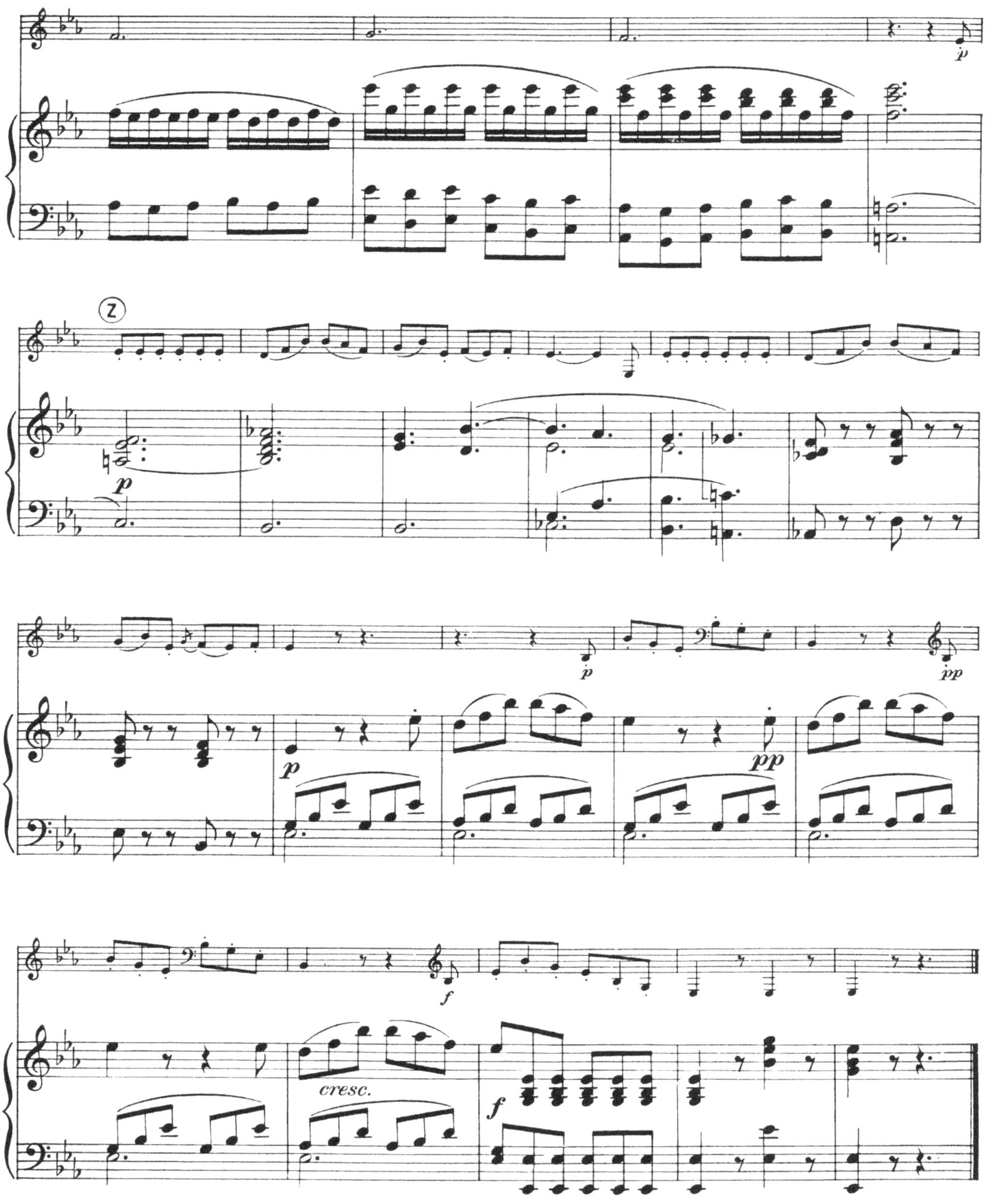
p
Z
p
p
pp
p
pp
f
cresc.
f

Concert Rondo

[K.371]

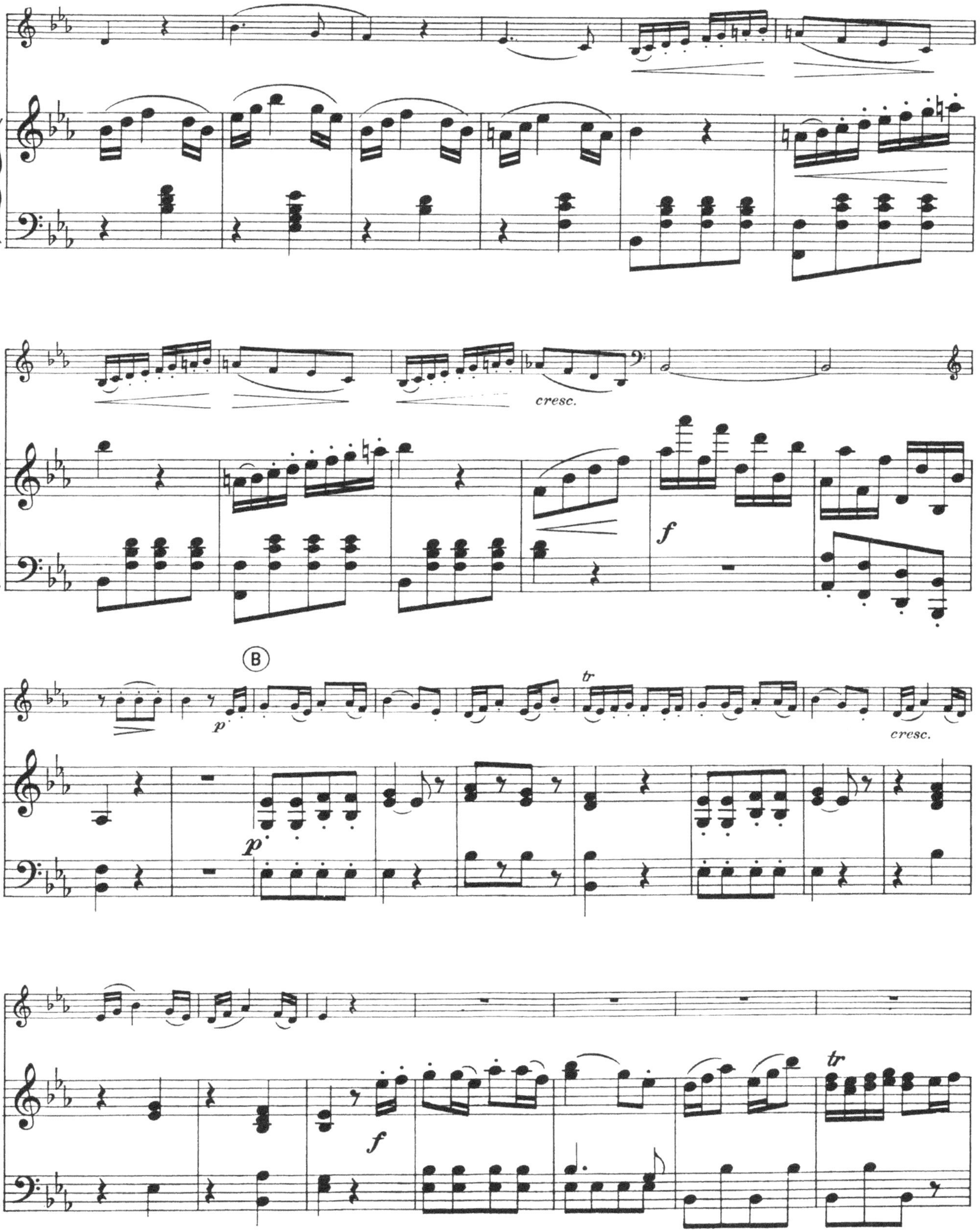
cresc.
f
B
p
tr
cresc.
f
tr

Concert Rondo

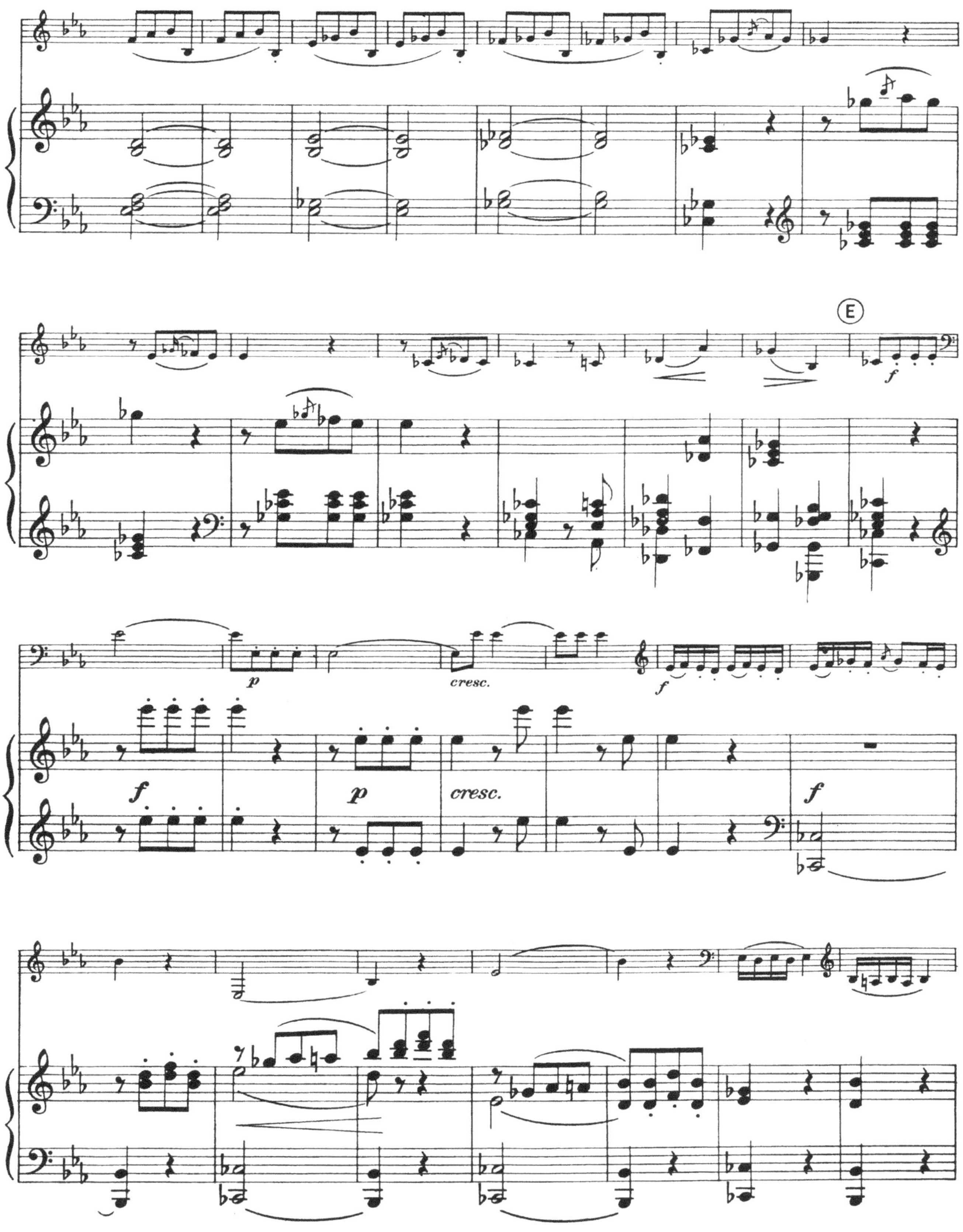
E
f
p
cresc.
f
p
cresc.
f

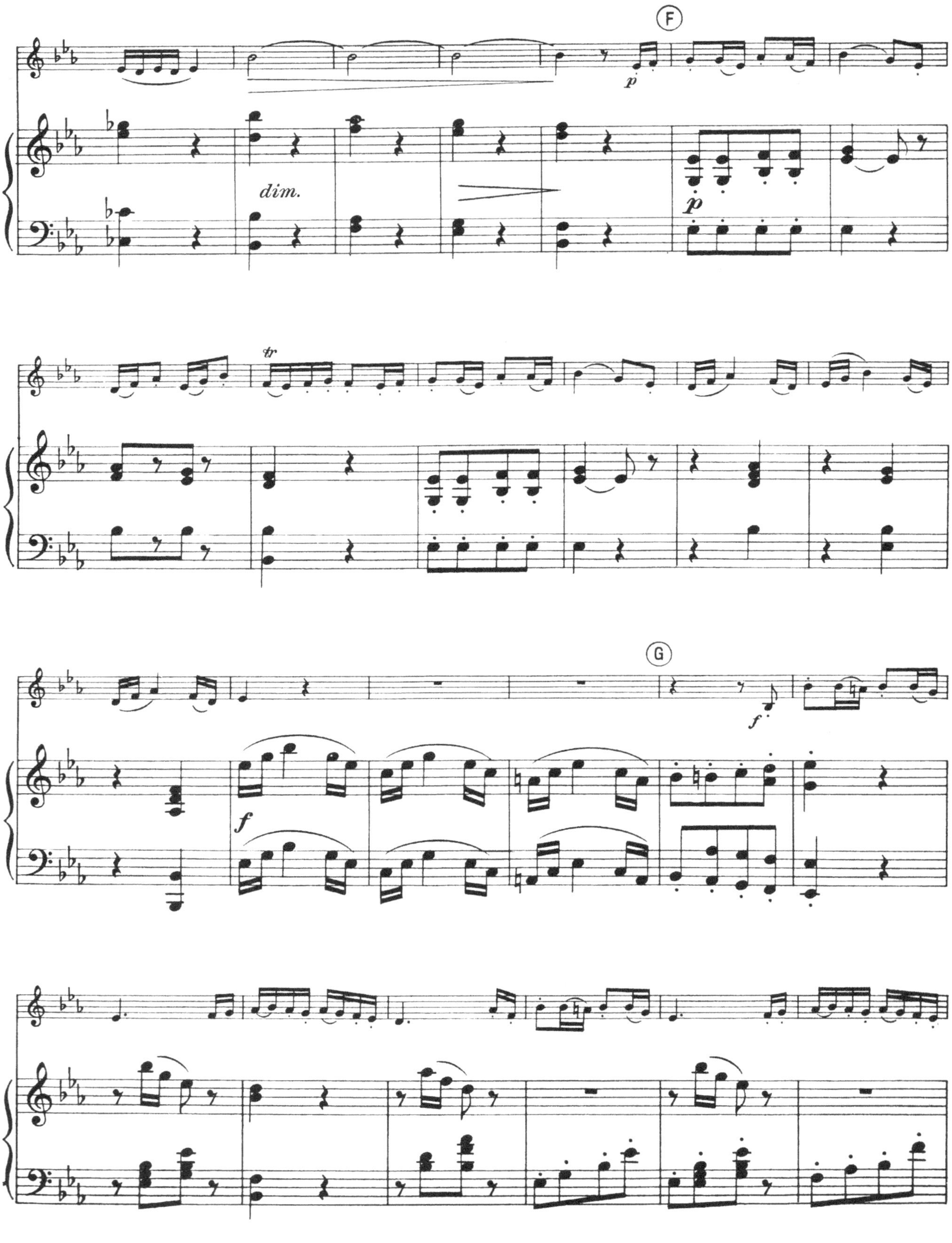
F
p
dim.
p
tr
G
f
f

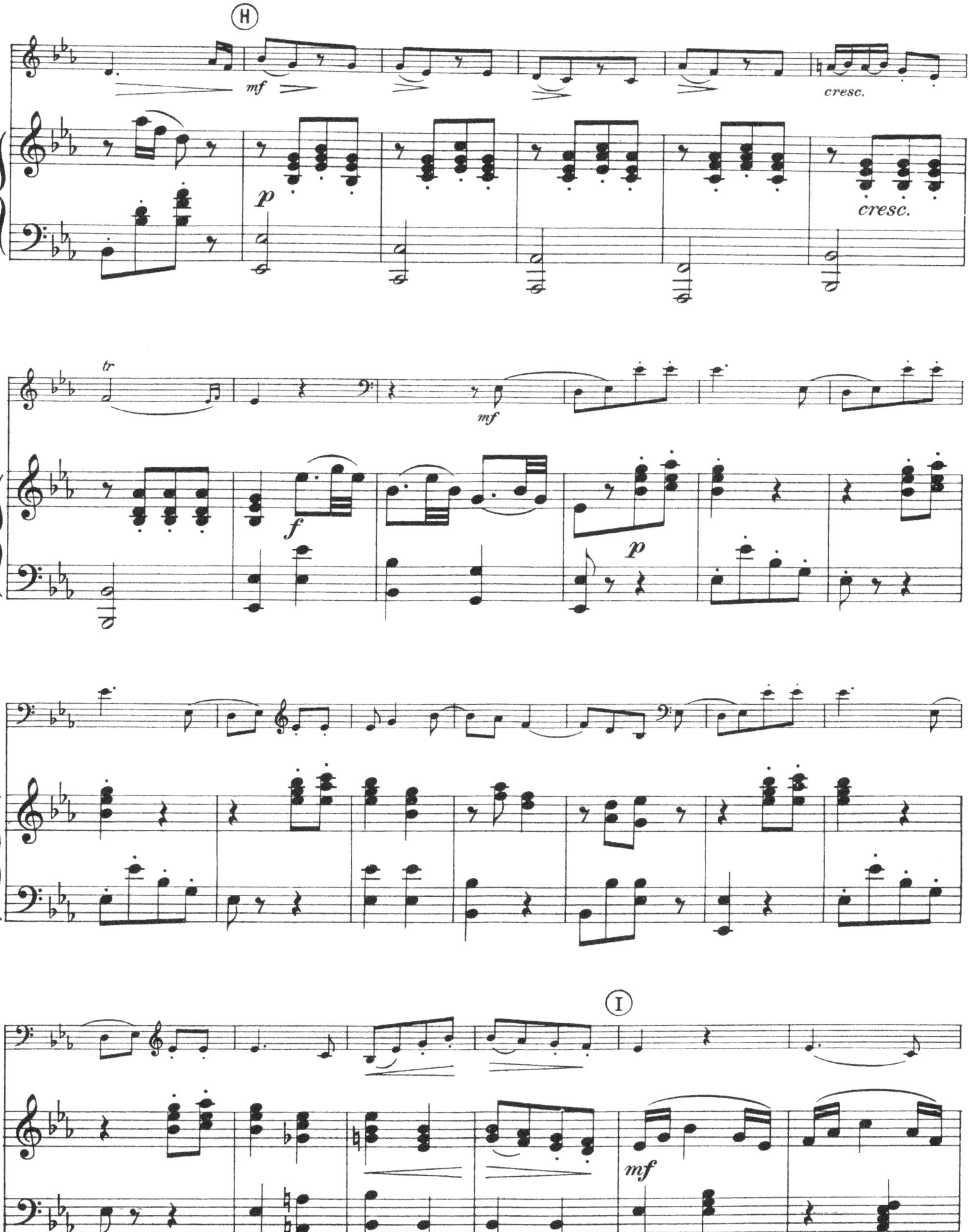
H
mf
cresc.
p
cresc.
tr
mf
f
p
I
mf

Concert Rondo

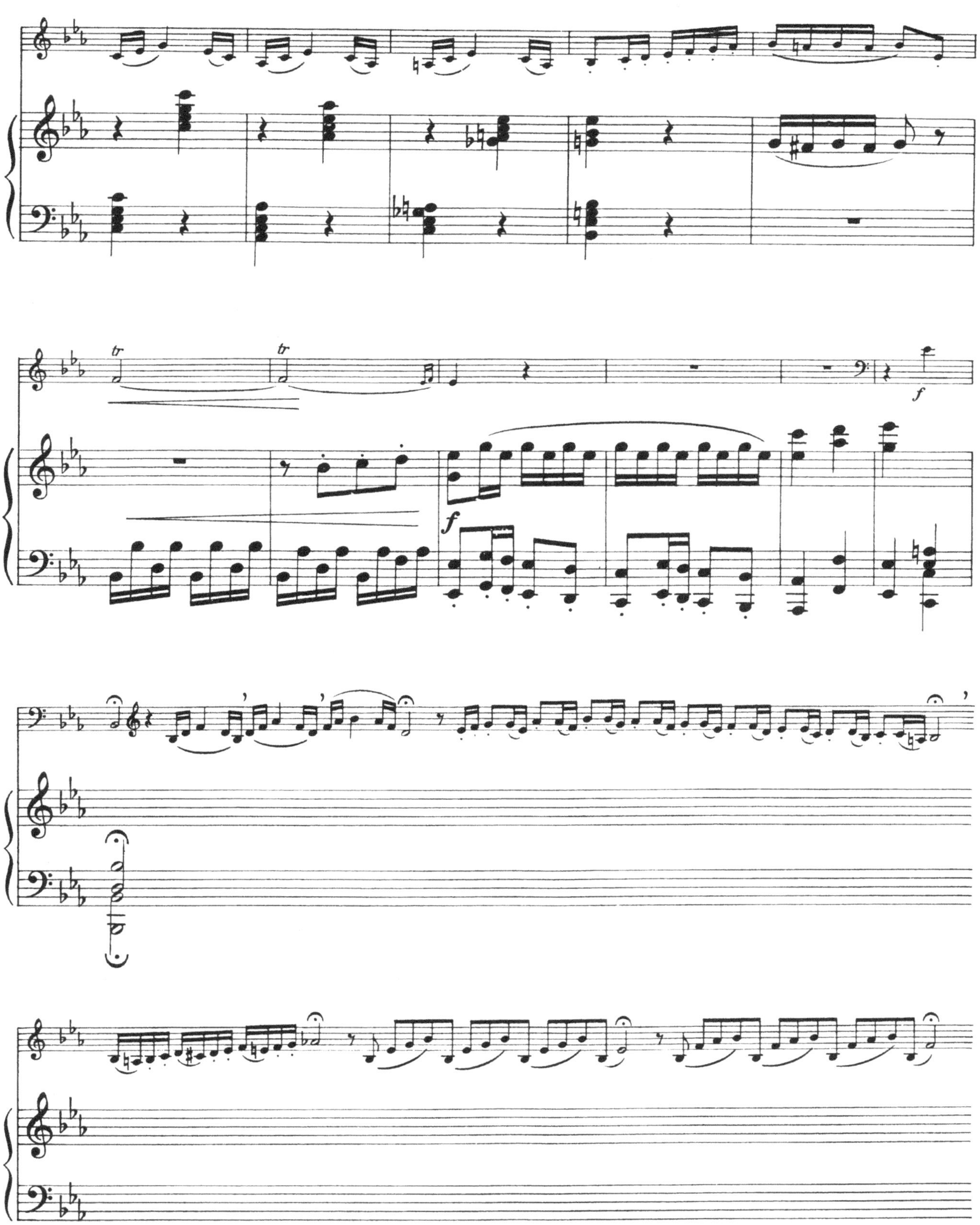

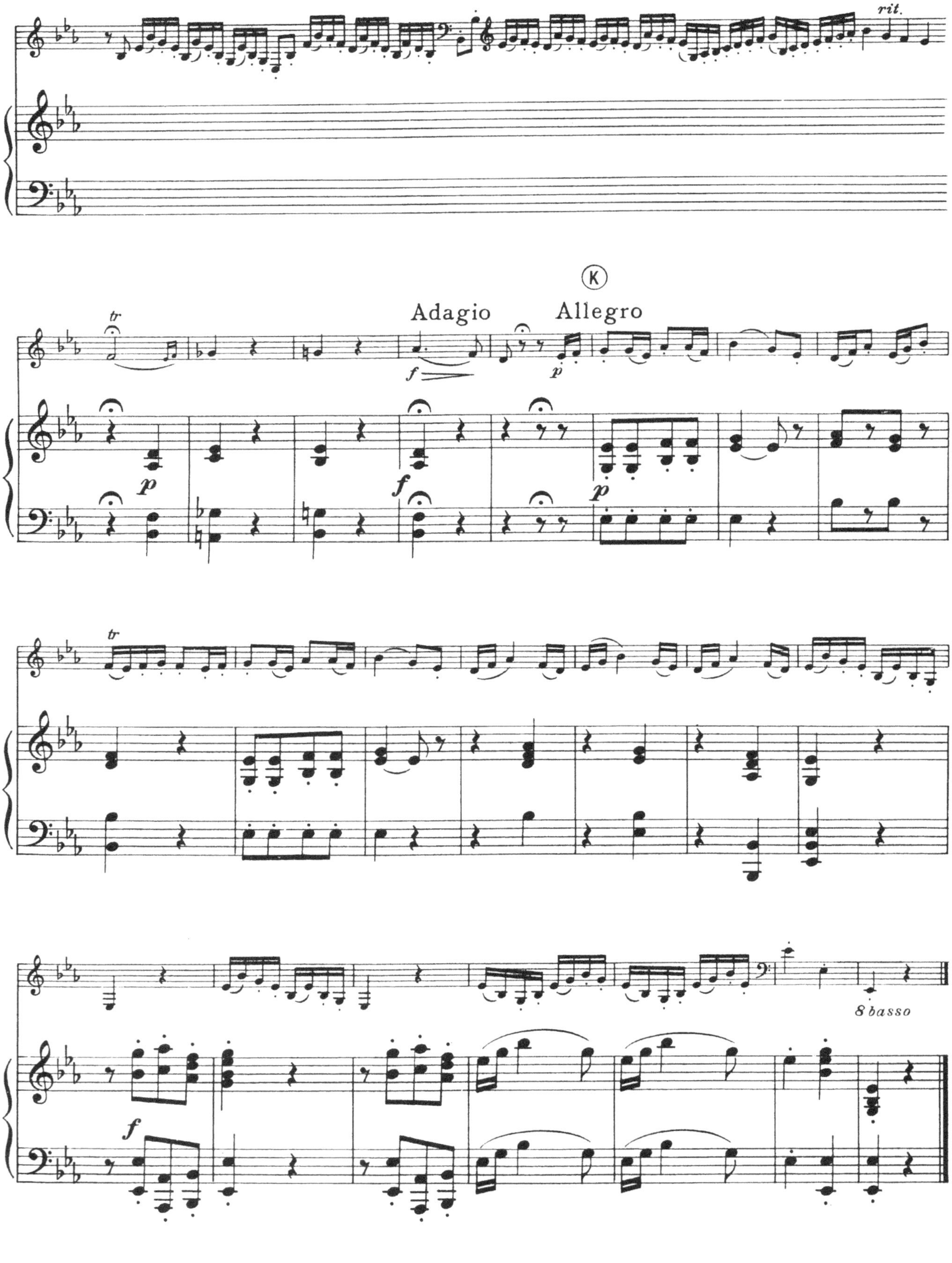
rit.
tr
K
Adagio
Allegro
f
p
8 basso